Off Grid Solar Power
&
Year Round Solar
Greenhouse

Small Footprint Press

STOP

BEFORE YOU START READING, DOWNLOAD YOUR FREE BONUSES!

Scan the QR-code & Access
all the Resources for FREE!

SCAN ME

The Self-Sufficient Living Cheat Sheet
10 Simple Steps to Become More Self-Sufficient in 1 Hour or Less

How to restore balance to the environment around you… even if you live in a tiny apartment in the city.
Discover:

- **How to increase your income** by selling "useless" household items
- The environmentally friendly way to replace your car — invest in THIS special vehicle to **eliminate your carbon footprint**
- The secret ingredient to **turning your backyard into a thriving garden**
- 17+ different types of food scraps and 'waste' that you can use to feed your garden
- How to drastically **cut down on food waste** without eating less
- 4 natural products you can use to make your own eco-friendly cleaning supplies
- The simple alternative to 'consumerism' — the age-old method for **getting what you need without paying money for it**
- The 9 fundamental items you need to create a self-sufficient first-aid kit
- One of the top skills that most people are afraid of learning — and how you can master it effortlessly
- 3 essential tips for **gaining financial independence**

The Prepper Emergency Preparedness & Survival Checklist:
10 Easy Things You Can Do Right Now to Ready Your Family & Home for Any Life-Threatening Catastrophe

Natural disasters demolish everything in their path, but your peace of mind and sense of safety don't have to be among them. Here's what you need to know...

- Why having an emergency plan in place is so crucial and how it will help to keep your family safe
- How to stockpile emergency supplies intelligently and why you shouldn't overdo it
- How to store and conserve water so that you know you'll have enough to last you through the crisis
- A powerful 3-step guide to ensuring financial preparedness, no matter what happens
- A step-by-step guide to maximizing your storage space, so you and your family can have exactly what you need ready and available at all times
- Why knowing the hazards of your home ahead of time could save a life and how to steer clear of these in case of an emergencyEverything you need to know for creating a successful evacuation plan, should the worst happen and you need to flee safely

101 Recipes, Tips, Crafts, DIY Projects and More for a Beautiful Low Waste Life
Reduce Your Carbon Footprint and Make Earth-Friendly Living Fun With This Comprehensive Guide

Practical, easy ways to improve your personal health and habits while contributing to a brighter future for yourself and the planet

Discover:
- **Simple customizable recipes for creating your own food, home garden, and skincare products**
- The tools you need for each project to successfully achieve sustainable living
- Step-by-step instructions for life-enhancing skills from preserving food to raising your own animals and forging for wild berries
- **Realistic life changes that reduce your carbon-footprint while saving you money**
- Sustainable crafts that don't require any previous knowledge or expertise
- Self-care that extends beyond the individual and positively impacts the environment
- **Essential tips on how to take back control of your life -- become self-sustained and independent**

First Aid Fundamentals

A Step-By-Step Illustrated Guide to the Top 10 Essential First Aid Procedures Everyone Should Know

Discover:

- **What you should do to keep this type of animal attack from turning into a fatal allergic reaction**
- Why sprains are more than just minor injuries, and how you can keep them from getting worse
- **How to make the best use of your environment in critical situations**
- The difference between second- and third-degree burns, and what you should do when either one happens
- Why treating a burn with ice can actually cause more damage to your skin
- When to use heat to treat an injury, and when you should use something cold
- **How to determine the severity of frostbite**, and what you should do in specific cases
- Why knowing this popular disco song could help you save a life
- The key first aid skill that everyone should know — **make sure you learn THIS technique the right way**

Food Preservation Starter Kit
10 Beginner-Friendly Ways to Preserve Food at Home |
Including Instructional Illustrations and Simple Directions

Grocery store prices are skyrocketing! It's time for a self-sustaining lifestyle.

Discover:

- **10 incredibly effective and easy ways to preserve your food for a self-sustaining lifestyle**
- The art of canning and the many different ways you can preserve food efficiently without any prior experience
- A glorious trip down memory lane to learn the historical methods of preservation passed down from one generation to the next
- **How to make your own pickled goods**: enjoy the tanginess straight from your kitchen
- Detailed illustrations and directions so you won't feel lost in the preservation process
- The health benefits of dehydrating your food and how fermentation can be **the key to a self-sufficient life**
- **The secrets to living a processed-free life** and saving Mother Earth all at the same time

Get all the resources for FREE by scanning
the QR-Code below:

Off Grid Solar Power & Year Round Solar Greenhouse

2-in-1 Compilation

Make Your Own Solar Power System and build Your Own Passive Solar Greenhouse Without Drowning in a Sea of Technical Jargon

Small Footprint Press

Table of Contents

YEAR ROUND SOLAR GREENHOUSE

OFF GRID SOLAR POWER

Year Round Solar Greenhouse

*Step-By-Step Guide to Design And Build Your
Own Passive Solar Greenhouse in as Little as
30 Days Without Drowning in a Sea
of Technical Jargon*

Small Footprint Press

Introduction

"The glorious lamp of heaven, the sun."

–by Robert Herrick

The world is just not what it used to be. Everyone knows this. Taking a look outside or a walk on the beach reflects the vast differences between today and ten years ago. Even going to a mall and checking out the food on the shelf will tell you a lot. Life has become so modernized, wiping out the existence of self-sustaining farms or gardens in exchange for massive, industrialized, and processed foods. Anyone who has grown their produce can show you the radical difference between plants grown by the earth and sun, untouched by chemicals in comparison to those in the shops—significantly smaller, tasteless, and pumped with substances whose damage is unknown.

You may have been inspired to take on gardening. You may have the desire to build your greenhouse to transform back into an individual who is self-sufficient, going against society's food standards in exchange for quality, fresh produce. You may also have a love for plants and a green thumb, enjoying the tranquility and joy that comes with gardening. It is certainly a rewarding experience, and now the future is truly at your fingertips. Greenhouse gardening is surely on another level than what is normally done, and its popularity is growing at a rapid rate.

Knowing where to start and what you need is tricky. You have probably heard of passive solar greenhouses and even considered trying it yourself, but without proper and updated guidance or care, there is a certain fear of failure. There are a lot of reasons for starting a greenhouse. Perhaps you want to be ensured that your plants will grow as well as have everything operating as smoothly as possible. You may have a tight budget and space. You may also want to build a greenhouse due to your harsh climate that does not allow the growth of plants in your normal hostile environment, where it rains too much or is far too cold. Wintertime might just be the bane of your existence, as it wipes out most of your plants in the frost and snow. You also want to be completely sure that your project will not fail.

This book acts as a constructive, helpful guide for anyone who wants to build a solar greenhouse in thirty days, going in-depth on how to build it as well as tips and tools for the building process. It is a helping hand and simplifies complicated instructions to make your DIY journey more straightforward and more enjoyable. It will tackle all issues you may encounter, such as budget constraints, climate concerns, choosing a type of greenhouse, ventilation, and more. It may sound like a lot, but the reward will be worth it. Not only will a solar greenhouse turn an environmentally hostile space into a plant-friendly haven, but it also will have a practical build to combat the different seasons that come across your path.

Small Footprint Press was born out of frustration with the

current state of the planet. Our mission is to help you sustainably survive and thrive while ensuring together that the world is a better place for future generations to come. Living more sustainably is a win for both humans and the environment, allowing the world to prosper alongside humanity. If more people went green, the world would be a happier, healthier, and more sustainable place, where one can see blue skies, clear waters, and a blooming ecosystem. A passive solar greenhouse combats the over industrialized and commercialized food system, where people are completely reliant on mass productions. However, with mass production comes mass waste. A greenhouse's very intention is to eliminate waste and recycle as much as possible.

The idea and inspiration to build a solar greenhouse brings you one step closer to creating a better world. It may seem insignificant to the actions of a single person. Yet, that is all it takes to instigate another's actions and ultimately building up a community of like-minded people. After all, you will be eating healthier foods and exposing yourself to higher levels of oxygen produced by your greenhouse in the long run.

Chapter 1:
What Is a Passive Solar Greenhouse?

Aesthetic Greenhouse

You may have a general idea of a solar greenhouse. The terms solar and greenhouse form an explanation in and of itself. Yet when going in detail, it can be pretty confusing or unclear. So, what exactly does it mean to have a passive solar greenhouse?

A passive solar greenhouse relies on two main factors: solar radiation and ideal growing conditions. Solar radiation is necessary for plants to create photosynthesis as well as survive. Plants need good conditions, such as constant temperature and humidity, to grow. An average greenhouse does manage to keep the conditions relatively the same, but, come winter, fuel is usually needed to keep up the sustenance. Energy is not only costly but also a high pollutant factor. Therefore, the average greenhouse might keep the pests away but is also bound to the seasons.

When a greenhouse is solar, the entire structure will heat up through the use of sunlight. It means that adding fuel is duly unnecessary. The passive solar greenhouse soaks in the sunlight during the winter season. Then, it will create proper heating and solar radiation for plants to thrive in the winter as they did in the summer.

Active Solar Greenhouse vs. Passive Solar Greenhouse

There are various types of greenhouses, but since we explicitly focus on passive solar greenhouses, it would be wise to know the difference between passive and active solar greenhouses. They are both solar, which means they derive and take energy from the sun. However, they also serve more designated purposes. Being solar-driven means that they can harness the power and store it for the colder nights and seasons.

These solar greenhouses can be classified into two different categories. One is known to be active, while the other is passive.

An active solar greenhouse tends to use extra energy. This means it moves the energy from a storage area to some other regions of an operational solar greenhouse.

However, a passive solar greenhouse tends to focus more on storing in preparation for the weather that tends to stay colder for longer. This is specifically ideal for people who want a cost-effective method to grow crops all year long.

Principles of Operation

There are some general principles on which a greenhouse operates. It first of all relies on the storage of solar energy that was accumulated through the day. The second step is where the greenhouse releases the energy gradually during the evening and winter.

A maximum amount of solar radiation (heat) is collected throughout the day and stored. Then, the heat is released into the interior. The loss of heat is reduced due to the insulation built inside the greenhouse. However, one also builds in ventilation to prevent overheating occurring. Therefore, it compensates for both extremes of heat and cold. However, it is a delicate balance, and this is where the science and tricky part comes in. Working out the balance is ultimately the key to creating a flourishing greenhouse, one whose temperature's swings at a reasonable rate to create a peaceful and amicable environment for plants to simply thrive. There are several steps a person can indeed take to achieve this.

Advantages of Passive Solar Greenhouses

To be motivated for a project such as this, it is best to understand what it brings to the table. A passive solar greenhouse is different from an average greenhouse for several reasons, bringing multiple benefits for you to enjoy.

- First, a passive solar greenhouse does absorb and release the necessary amount of solar radiation for the photosynthesis process that needs to occur for plants. The plants need a good amount of sunlight to survive properly.

- A significant reduction in heat loss considering a greenhouse has thick, triple-layered walls built-in from north, west, and east sides. This helps to keep the plants nice and cozy during the winter.

- There is constant sustenance of the climatic conditions in the house. It means a person is capable of growing vegetables all year round regardless of the weather. This factor saves a lot of time and reduces the need to always visit the grocery store for certain vegetables when it is out of season. For people who love gardening, this is ideal, considering they do not have to wait to plant their seeds nor struggle to grow what they want to.

- It is also an income possibility, especially if you are in a rural population selling your fresh produce. You may be surprised how many people would instead opt for homegrown produce rather than those sold in the local store, as they are fresher, healthier, and certainly not pumped with excessive chemicals.

- The design and build of a passive solar greenhouse are practical, built alongside the east-west axis (later explained in the book), which allows the greenhouse to soak in the sun for the most prolonged period.

- Any needs for specific vegetables that are not ordinarily sustainable or capable of being grown can be fulfilled in a passive solar greenhouse. For example, if you would like to produce foods that cannot even typically be grown in your country, it is quite possible to do so in a greenhouse.

- The materials necessary to create a passive solar greenhouse are, on average, locally available. Considering it is made out of straw, wood, and stone.

The only abnormality would be the transparent glass or cover sheet, which happens to cover the south side of the wall. These are called glazings and are an essential aspect of your greenhouse.

- The greenhouse doesn't need special licensed people to build it. If you know enough about construction or want to hire a local builder, you are more than welcome. The only people you may need to call in are licensed plumbers or electricians only if absolutely need be.

- The original investment costs can be recovered after three years if the production is managed professionally and the product is sold. Otherwise, you can consider the money you are saving from not going grocery shopping as a return of investment.

- The costs are relatively modest. It all depends on what and how you install it. You can undoubtedly opt for cheap options to even recycling items that you already have.

- The heat source relies entirely on the sun and material to heat the water and hold material such as concrete. The energy source is altogether economical as well as accessible. You will be cutting a lot of costs of fuel and electricity from simply building a solar greenhouse. However, if your climate is known to be abnormally frigid with little sun exposure, you may have to compensate a little for that. So this benefit does depend entirely on where you stay.

Four Main Elements of a Passive Solar Greenhouse

To understand the basics of a passive solar greenhouse, you need to know the four main elements of the greenhouse. They are the foundational building blocks and the keys to success. Therefore, when planning to build your greenhouse, these are by far the elements you need to consider first and plan in detail before moving to actual construction.

Orientation

The first element is orientation. This is the greenhouse position to reach maximum exposure to the sun for the most extended period possible. The design starts with choosing the proper orientation of your greenhouse. If you are in the Northern Hemisphere, it means you need to maximize the exposure of your greenhouse on the southern side. Whereas if you are in the southern hemisphere, you need to maximize the exposure on the northern side of the house.

If you are in the northern hemisphere, then the north side of your greenhouse will collect the minimum amount of light. That is why some rooms in a house are colder than others. Therefore it is best to focus on insulating that side as best as you can in order to reduce the amount of heat loss that may occur. This might seem like common knowledge when building your greenhouses, yet there are still some questions and confusion that could arise when you are busily orientating your greenhouse.

The best location for your greenhouse is where there is full access to light, but it does need shade as well. Shading is not so important in the summer, where the trees can protect the greenhouse from the sun's harsh heat, but those same trees may block vital rays in the winter. This does mean it is better to build your greenhouse close to deciduous trees. Trees that lose their leaves in the winter, reducing the amount of shading, but helping it out in the summer when the leaves do grow back. While trees are useful for shading, you do not need to build next to trees, as you can easily install your own shading if necessary.

You also need to make sure your greenhouse is quite easily accessible. Consider that greenhouses do need a certain level of attention, so please do yourself a huge favor and build in an easily accessible location.

A southwest-facing greenhouse can potentially overheat due to the sun having additional time in the afternoon, which happens to be the hottest part of the day. It really does depend on your climate, however, and if it does get frigid, then those extra rays of the sun will always help. However, on average, it is better not to build your passive solar greenhouse in this position. Otherwise, you may be finding yourself overspending on ventilation and shading.

If you happen to have a sloped hillside explicitly facing the south, it is a perfect spot for your greenhouse. The earth that faces the north will act as added protection and insulation, but it does ask for more effort in time and a more complicated process. For example, you will need to build a well-structured north wall that can handle the extra pressure of the downward-facing soil.

Insulation

There is a massive reduction in heating costs and higher efficiency when a greenhouse is adequately insulated. The colder the climate you are in, the more critical it certainly gets by far. Proper insulation will act as a way of saving your plants and cut down on all the energy a person would need to spend trying to maintain a specific temperature.

It would be best if you considered several factors while choosing your style of insulation, such as your location, climate and amount of ventilation provided, etc. You will also need to consider the amount of light transmission, considering that the thicker your polycarbonate, the less light you will receive. There is no use in insulating a greenhouse when you cannot get in the proper light and heat for the plants in the first place. You will also learn how to calculate how much insulation you need and want through R-value.

Ventilation

One of the essential components of a greenhouse's success is ventilation. If a person does not have the proper ventilation, the greenhouses and the plants inside will face a storm of problems. Proper ventilation serves four different primary purposes inside of a greenhouse. It helps if the temperature is regulated. It also assists with giving your plants plenty of fresh air in which they can photosynthesize. Finally, good ventilation prevents pest infestations and will help to encourage pollination, which is crucial inside a greenhouse. If you find that your plants are struggling, the first thing you may need to consider is improving the ventilation in your greenhouse.

Looking at temperature, it may surprise you to know that more plants tend to die due to excess heat inside of a greenhouse rather than the cold. Many plants genuinely are sensitive to heat and could wilt. It is best to place vents throughout the greenhouse considering the greenhouse will better regulate the temperature and allow some heat to escape naturally. If your climate is sweltering, then you should consider using an evaporative cooler alongside an exhaust fan to keep your greenhouse cool in many hot climates.

Fresh air is desperately needed for plants to photosynthesize. Considering they need carbon dioxide for food. If the greenhouse lacks good airflow, your plants may not be able to produce as many sugars for their food. This could result in plants struggling as well as dying, so make sure the plants can breathe.

Ventilation helps with pests. It is an odd realization, but poor ventilation does cause plants to become sick. This means they will become targets or attractions to bugs. So keep those fans spinning.

Lastly, there is pollination to keep in mind. A good wind helps for pollination to occur in nature, making a substitute for it within a greenhouse is essential. Moving air will gently shake the plants that help pollination to occur. This is important for plants such as tomatoes which are known to be self-pollinating. A good rule of thumb to remember is that if you see that your plants are not fruiting, you need to add to the level of airflow within your greenhouse. Gentle airflow will also encourage your plants to grow sturdier root systems and stems. The airflow will overall improve the plants' health.

Temperature Regulation and Climate Control

Considering temperature does play an important role, it is only natural to understand the regulation of temperatures to adapt to a climate. A standard greenhouse does require an excess of heating as well as cooling during the changing of environments. It does make it harder to grow the best, fresh local foods when it is not within its season. The solar greenhouse's every intention is to build an energy-efficient greenhouse that is self-sustainable when it comes to temperature control. There are specific strategies that a person would have to undertake when building the greenhouse. The most popular method solar greenhouses regulate temperature is through thermal mass. Thermal masses are known to be dense materials that have the ability to store a large amount of energy (heat). They are placed in the sun, heating up during the day and slowly releasing it during the night. Water is known to be the oldest and the most common form for this. Generally, there are significant water barrels stacked on the northern side, which helps to make a dramatic reduction in fluctuating temperatures.

However, a new and more practical method has arisen which uses the soil underground. It is a free and valuable resource.

The earth can be used for thermal energy as well as act as a method of stabilization for temperatures within a greenhouse. In essence, it works like water but does not take up half the space that water barrels do. It also provides more heat and has a more consistent temperature attached to it. This is typically called a climate battery or a Ground Air Heat Transfer system (GAHT) if one wants to be fancy.

In summary, it heats up during the day as hot air gets pumped to the pipes, which are buried underground as is inevitably transferred to the soil, then in the evening, the cooler, drier air transports the heat back into the greenhouse. This is the basic idea of a climate battery and, in reality, far more practical and cheaper than water. The climate battery, along with other forms of thermal mass, will be discussed later in this book.

Now that you understand the different steps and elements to build a successful solar power greenhouse, one can only wonder what steps a person should take to start. This is the beginning of a fantastic journey for you, as well as incredibly rewarding. Now that you have some of the foundational knowledge, it is time to expand it further. You will be exposed to various options and ideas to follow through on, and don't be afraid of the variety. The more variety you have, the better you can choose and build a perfectly tailored greenhouse to your environment, space, and budget.

Chapter 2:
Before You Begin

You are excited to get started. Who wouldn't be? A project this size with enormous potential will have anyone itching to start. Yet, a person needs to be prepared. Planning and preparation are critical, after all. Without them, you are destined to fail or build yourself a poor-quality greenhouse anyhow. So here are a few things you need to consider even before you start to develop your passive solar greenhouse.

Location

As mentioned before, location is essential. Next, you need to consider the orientation of the greenhouse. Consider this, your passive solar greenhouse, in all intents and purposes, is a solar collector in order to encourage plants to thrive in the heat and photosynthesis. The ideal orientation for a greenhouse is to be -15 degrees to the east or south. This applies when you are in the Northern hemisphere. The opposite applies to those who are in the southern hemisphere. This helps to optimize the amount of morning light it receives as well as the heat when the greenhouse is at its coldest. However, if you have limited options, you can still orient it about 45 degrees off south and still get a great result. In order to fully calculate this, consider using a solar pathfinder. It really doesn't take any batteries and is a great tool to assess and understand the solar resource throughout the entirety of the year. You can also use a solar pathfinder app on both Android or iOS if you would prefer a digital option. Make sure when choosing the site that there is not an excess of shading caused by buildings or trees. A solar greenhouse tends to need as much sun as possible.

Another issue may arise that you cannot build a greenhouse that faces south wholly. However, making it to face southwest (although not entirely recommended) or southeast would still be doable. It is preferable to build it southeast because it helps to heat up the greenhouse faster as the morning sunrises. Moments before dawn are always the coldest, which can certainly assist and help with plants waking up early in the morning.

Climate

Cold Climate

You need to think logically and assess the climate you are in. Is it ordinarily cold weather that occasionally warms up in the summer? Is it blistering hot with a heated winter? Or is it both? Do your research to find out about the climate in which the plants you intend to grow normally thrive. This will all play a role in the insulation and design of your greenhouse. For example, different plants thrive better in the cold, whereas others prefer heat. They all are different and unique in their particular way, and you do need to remember this. Although your greenhouse can practically host any plant depending on how you build it, it might not cover the entire variety that you would want to plant. Instead, set it in different categories, where the maximum of plants that suit a similar environment are the focus in your greenhouse.

You can consider using a USDA tool online to figure out the minimum and maximum temperatures in the area you currently live in. Then, search the temperatures from the climate you would like to mimic the zones you live in, specifically the common plants you are interested in. Even if they are plants around your area, then you can focus on the season in which it grows and flourishes.

Furthermore, there is a tool online you can use to find the best plants for each of the USDA zones, which you can easily find online or by asking plant shops.

Figuring all these out is vital for later calculations that will need to be made. Figuring out your climate is a practical step for working out your ventilation and insulation.

Budget

If you can't afford the cost, unfortunately, it can't be built. Therefore, it is generally a good idea to budget and prepare yourself for rough estimates about the design, materials, and other elements that come inside your greenhouse. On the other hand, it is never a good idea to walk in and purchase items blindly, only to be baffled at the massive bill that comes your way. So, here are some questions to ask yourself:

- What is the amount you are looking to spend?

- And what are the average costs of all the equipment?

- Are there items I would like to save up for?

- Are there tools I can purchase and attach later?

- When does quality over quantity truly matter?

Local Regulation

It is all good and well to build a greenhouse until you are fined and forced to take it down due to a lack of a permit. There are bound to be greenhouse building regulations, and each one would vary from area to area. This is all to make sure the buildings are safe and suited for the environment. So, what are the regulations in your specific location? Do you need zoning or a building permit? It all depends on where you live. However, it should not be too exceedingly challenging to gain a license for a greenhouse, considering its practical nature.

There are two types of permits you need to consider when building a greenhouse. They are known as zoning and building permits.

Zoning permits are found through the local zoning department to see precisely what is required. They regulate where precisely the location of the greenhouse is allowed on the property. It usually means there will be specified plotlines in which you are permitted to build. Whether it is by the side, end, or front is all determined by your community regulations. It also may regulate the number of accessories that you are allowed on your property. Items, such as sheds or other forms of outbuildings, could be considered accessories as well as the size of your building. Specifically sized greenhouses might not even need a zoning permit, but it is all best to do your research and find that out at your local department. Staying both eco-friendly and legal within the laws of your area.

County building departments issue building permits. There are structural codes given to have a peek at both the integrity of the structure and the physical appearance. If you live in a rural area, there is usually no need for permits to build accessory buildings, but most urban areas have at least some requirements. Either way, play it safe and find out. No harm is done by doing a little extra research before starting on a big project like this, especially if the consequences are quite significant.

The building codes typically tackle structural integrity issues and deal with potential weather problems such as wind or snow, depending on the location of your area. Unfortunately, attaching your greenhouse will also be likely to require a permit, just because they are indeed considered to be an addition to your home.

Usually, building codes deal with attached greenhouses in quite a similar fashion as a sunroom. In addition, there are codes to deal with the appearance of the building, which will be different for each community. Some have high levels of aesthetics, while others might be more lenient. However, it is uncommon for communities to disapprove of greenhouses. On the contrary, they usually are welcomed with open arms and encouraged from time to time. You might even find your neighbors coming in asking for tips at the end of the day.

You can also consider getting the help of experienced and local greenhouse manufacturers who are all too aware of the regulation process. They could even help you apply for specific variances and assist you with discussing your plans to groups such as the homeowner's association, as it is their job to stay up to date. They are likely far more aware of the rules than the average communities surrounding them. Even if you are building your greenhouse and not hiring them, what harm is there to find your own information from them?

Common Mistakes to Avoid

A big part of the preparation is to ensure any and all mistakes are avoided when building a passive solar greenhouse. Being aware of the common mistakes people make from the start would certainly help your preparation. Considering many greenhouses have been built over the years, people have made a lot of mistakes.

Humidity

Firstly, be aware of humidity in your greenhouse. Too much humidity will allow mold spores and diseases to grow crazy and fester in your greenhouse. On the other hand, a certain amount of humidity is to be expected. Otherwise, your plants are bound to die of thirst. Therefore it is best to do your research on the plants you want, grouping them according to their humidity needs. It's even better if perhaps you can grow them at the same time. This, however, entirely depends on the amount of space you have in your greenhouse. A good and common way to add to the humidity is through misting, which will be discussed a little later in the book.

Shade

As much as a solar greenhouse is built to soak in the sun, certain plants still need shade, even if it is in the middle of winter! It is wise to consider getting a few greenhouse covers to help shade plants. This is especially helpful in the heat of the day when certain plants need a little fewer rays and a little more darkness. Otherwise, your plants could die from overexposure. It does depend entirely on the plant, as some are designed for as much sun as possible, whereas others may even require shade full time (which means rather grow it in your house if need be). In a greenhouse, plants certainly should be able to survive on a certain amount of exposure to the sun.

There are various shading materials you can get in DIY stores, even online, if need be. You can decide to pull them over the roof and set up an automated system. Or you can opt for the cheaper version and aim for something manual.

Heating

Heating is important and will be covered in-depth later in this book. Consider how the temperature drops at night and how different it is from the day. These fluctuations can damage plants. Frost is a deadly and formidable winter foe that destroys plants literally overnight. It is not recommended for you to use an average house heater for the greenhouse. Quite a few people have done this, and as convenient as it may seem, placing a heater inside your greenhouse is like placing a heater outside. It is just not made for the humidity nor the environment. It is best to use heaters specifically designed for the greenhouse itself or opt for the passive heating methods for a solar passive greenhouse. That is entirely up to you.

Plant Choice

A lot of mistakes are made in the choice of plants. Considering they are the very reason you want to build a greenhouse, it is important to grow the right plants as well. This doesn't mean you are limited, but rather that you need to plan ahead in order to design your greenhouse for the plants you desire. It's good to compile a list of plants you would like to grow and then consider the amount of space, height, and even soil. Some plants are inconsiderate of other plants and may grow too tall (overshadowing other smaller plants) or even aggressively taking over. Believe it or not, some plants do have turf wars. They may be very slow turf wars, but regardless some plants are more aggressive than others, and it is best to be aware of plant behaviors. If other plants grow to the point that they come into contact with the greenhouse covering, they themselves could become root causes for disease, mildew, and even mold growth! Picking your plant is not that much different from picking a pet, after all, it may seem.

Soil Choice

Soil is another common mistake made where people opt to

fill their containers with garden soil. Yet this is likely to turn out into a major disaster. Soil normally tends to get compacted, in easier terms, "squished," where the bottom of the container has all the water, and the top is dry. They are not designed to be in pots, after all.

You should rather consider using potting soils and steer clear from garden soils. This makes all the difference in the world. Make sure not to mix them up either, as the temptation may be there to mix cheaper soil with more costly ones to spread them out further. There is a popular practice to grow your plants in something called peat moss or coir. Coir is also known as coconut fiber.

Wrong Fertilizer

As much as people may grab a random bag of fertilizer for their plants, research has to be done even when it comes to these kinds of things. Plants are much like pets in which they have certain requirements in order to survive. However, unlike certain pets, plants can actually be more finicky and may even need something different than your standard one size fits all kind of fertilizer. Much like anything else in life, there is no magical singular formula or soil for all the plants in the world.

So again, grouping your plants to have similar water, fertilizer and shade will save you a lot of trouble, effort, and time. You can even consider adding a certain marker system as an indicator for your plant's requirements, etc. You can add markers for water and stickers, perhaps even for fertilizer, allowing you to have a greater understanding of your plants' needs without having to google it all the time.

A lot of these mistakes may seem obvious, yet when the time comes to build a greenhouse, you may be surprised how often it happens. So take your time in your planning and preparation, as well as learning about the various elements of a successful passive solar greenhouse.

Best Tips Before Building Your Greenhouse

Before building a greenhouse, there are few things to keep in mind. This is to help your preparation and success in the long run. First, you need to have a full understanding of the reasons why you want to build one. Most people tend to have a greenhouse because gardening is amongst the top hobbies in the world. Because building your greenhouse will take time, patience, and maintenance, it is best to make sure you want to build a greenhouse and care for it. It is a commitment you have to make. Here are most of the popular reasons, and make sure it is important enough for you to keep going.

Having a greenhouse allows you to plant all season. Therefore, there is no concern about planting vegetables in the winter, as you are practically in the perfect environment to grow everything.

You do end up saving money, cutting out the costs of plants, lawns, and seeds for the spring season. You will have the ability to grow your own seeds as well as give them away to friends and family. You are also using the space around you for a reason. If you build a large enough greenhouse, you might not even need a gardening shed, as you can store everything you need alongside growing the plants as well. This brings multipurpose and has you being far more efficient with your space.

The greenhouse will also protect the plants from the weather as well as pest infestations. Pests are a very common problem and amongst the main causes of crop failure. Whether it be caterpillars, spider mites, and even locusts, your conservatories keep your plants healthy and happy.

You also do need to consider the cost. How much are you truly willing to invest in your greenhouse? Considering this is a DIY book, you will be shaving a lot of money from other professionals, but it does mean you will have to gather the materials yourself and budget well. Some costs may end up being more than you realized, and even for that, you do need to be prepared. Always have a little buffer to help for expenditures you may not have seen coming.

When it comes to a DIY solar passive greenhouse, you can use pretreated wood, steel, aluminum, or even old windows to help build a greenhouse frame. Recycling is very much possible, and you can even ask your friends, family, and community if they have any unwanted items to get rid of. You can even consider visiting a recycling center or a flea market to fetch some of the materials.

Keeping Pests Out

Although greenhouses are meant to keep pests out, there are

still a few things to keep in mind to prevent pests from slipping in, as this is still a possibility that you sorely want to avoid.

Firstly, after you have built a greenhouse, it is best to inspect the plants you bring in very carefully. Look for any adult insects or even eggs, basically any signs of infestation. If you are suspicious of a certain plant, then consider treating it with pesticide before moving it into your greenhouse.

Secondly, it is best to install a good screen for all the openings you have in your greenhouse. This does include your vents and behind attached fans. Any screens that have an approximate 1/10 inch should keep out most of those nasty pests.

Thirdly, you really need to consider fitting a heavy-duty plastic floor or making sure the base is properly sealed. This will prevent insects from crawling under the walls.

Lastly, it is recommended to keep the area around your greenhouse completely free of any other plants or debris. It was considered that this could be the very item drawing in the bugs in the first place. So, it is just better to have some gravel or plain ground.

Best Tools for Building a Greenhouse

Much like an artist needs a pencil and a canvas so does a DIY greenhouse need a tool kit of their own. Here are some of the items you will need (apart from the materials mentioned in the book). As someone who is already dabbling in DIY and

DIY construction, you should hopefully have some of this equipment.

- Long-nosed pliers
- Nut spinners (size depends on what nuts you do use)
- Safety gloves
- Safety glasses
- Screwdriver
- Retractable knife
- A heavy-duty suction cup (especially if you use glass glazing)

The rest does depend on what you plan to do and build. Normally hammers, shovels, and other common construction equipment may be found necessary. Now, you are not required to purchase all the tools. In fact, you could even ask to borrow them from your neighbors temporarily. Then, all you need to do is make sure you have the tool on the day you actually need it. Otherwise, it can slow down your production.

A lot of these are important when planning your passive solar greenhouse. The last thing you want is to build a successful greenhouse and have it infested with bugs from the very beginning. So spare yourself the pain and trouble by planning just a little ahead.

Preparation is key. Without a plan, you are planning to fail. Therefore, it is best to get things right the first time and spare yourself much grief and costs.

Chapter 3:
The Greenhouse Shell and
Foundations

Every house that gets built needs to start somewhere. It would be an incredibly odd sight to see someone building a house roof first, then the walls and windows, and finishing the tiles last. Here you will need to make some critical decisions on the overall shell and design of the greenhouse alongside making wise decisions regarding the foundation of a greenhouse. The foundation plays a role in every structure or building you see. However, depending on your choice can also depend on whether you even have a foundation! Alongside the foundation, you need to work out the greenhouse's shell or framework too.

Attached vs. Detached Greenhouse

You may wonder whether or not a greenhouse should be attached or detached. Here are a few pointers for you to consider when securing a greenhouse.

Greenhouse With an Insulated Wall

If you attach your northern or southern side, it will provide a solid wall that is practically already insulated and adds excellent protection for the greenhouse. It certainly makes it more accessible for yourself if you add it to your house and easier to hook up electrical and water accessories. It can also act as a source of passive heat for your house, especially if it is connected to your house by an opening or a door. This works very well for homes that are already using solar heating for indoor thermal heating. However, in a standard home, a person needs to be cautious with glazing to not make too much heat loss or gain. It is also a stunning addition to your house, primarily if you focus on an aesthetically pleasing design. If you also want to spend a lot of time gardening and tending to your plants, this is also a good idea. Especially in winter, it is pretty horrible having to venture back and forth outside in the cold in comparison to only having to walk in and out of a room in your house.

However, some disadvantages of having it attached are a dense humid environment that could condense on any surface. This means that the side exposed to your greenhouses needs to have the ability to handle humidity. So, make sure you learn how to protect your items from humidity damage. It would be best to make sure that everything is waterproof to a certain degree and won't gain mold or rust, or even rot. This is especially a big concern if the wood is involved. It would help if you made sure the wood is treated with anti-rot and can handle the humidity coming its way.

Building another structure on your home may require you to obtain a permit to alter the already existing system. The rules can be far more strict than simply building an undetached greenhouse, as unfair as that may seem.

If you do want to have the look of an attached greenhouse

while avoiding certain building restrictions, you could consider building your greenhouse merely a couple of feet from the main structure and create a false wall between the two of them. This does, however, still require you to check with your county to discover the offset restrictions. You could even consider simply making a small walkway between the greenhouse and the main building if need be. Do your best to find out as much as possible about the regulations to stay legal and out of unnecessary trouble.

Space, Aspect Ratio, and Shape

If it doesn't fit, you can't build it. That may seem obvious, but it is easy to get measurements, plans, and ideas wrong precisely when it comes to fittings like glazing. You really want to make sure you get the aspect ratio right. Details matter in this case. Consider this as the footprint of your greenhouse. In order to maximize your solar gain and minimize the loss of thermal heat, it is generally better to have long, narrow, rectangular buildings. You can alter these slightly to make sure it fits in the size and location you have planned for it. Making your greenhouse rectangular will save you a lot of trouble and make your project a little easier.

The shape of your greenhouse is the 3D plan for the building. There are a wide variety of shapes available, but each and every one of them will have its advantages and drawbacks tacked alongside. Here are some of the basic principles you can use to decide the shape, also called your greenhouse's cross-section.

How high does the greenhouse need to be to grow the plants you want? Some plants are naturally taller than others, like tomatoes in comparison to carrots, for example. Some tomato plants can reach relatively high, whereas an average carrot should have more space in the soil.

Where would the lower and upper vent walls go? This all comes down to airflow, which is covered later.

Are there any height restrictions that you do need to be aware of? For example, if you are a tall person and would like to spend considerable time in the greenhouse, the last thing you want to do is constantly bump your head. Yet if you need to reach the roof for other various reasons, then you may want to make it reachable enough.

Is there any form or function that you would like to add to the greenhouse that may require specific overall shape adjustments? This could be the roof or the wall to which you want to attach your greenhouse too.

And what are the ergonomic requirements which you want in your greenhouse? Suppose you do not know what ergonomics is. In that case, it is known as the art of identifying flaws in the production process to avoid any significant inefficiencies from occurring. Thus, it is paying attention to detail, and this is undoubtedly necessary when building a greenhouse.

The moment you have figured out the aspect ratio (the practical ratio between the height and width of your greenhouse) as well as the cross-section (architectural drawings making it three-dimensional), then you have your overall shell design of your passive solar greenhouse.

Kneewall

Common Example of a Kneewall

So what exactly is a kneewall? What part does it happen to play in a greenhouse? A kneewall is the vertical front wall of the greenhouse that happens to be the support of the lower vent system. It works like a sandwich and is traditionally built like a house wall. It is typically recommended to construct a kneewall as thick as you can manage as well as afford. Kneewalls help by keeping the best forms of insulation inside of the greenhouse. It certainly helps to prevent heat from escaping. It is an essential component that sets explicitly out the height at the front of the greenhouse. It also has vertical space that allows snow to slide off the glazing to prevent too much accumulation.

It may be astounding to know that greenhouses need open front vents, even if it is the middle of winter, especially if it is on a sunny day. A person needs to ensure the vents do not get blocked up by snow. It is also best to build the kneewall about three to four feet high (Avis, 2018b). However, if your environment is prone to a high level of snowfall, you would have to consider making it larger or simply clearing the snow every now and then.

Roof

A roof is an obvious addition to the greenhouse. Yet, there is a little more to it than may initially meet the eye. When it comes to solar greenhouses, science and math are frequently involved in creating a flourishing plant-friendly environment. When it comes to roofs, it is all about the angles... literally! The way the sun hits your greenhouse makes quite a big difference. Most people don't really consider lighting or these aspects. Yet when building a passive solar greenhouse, it should be amongst your primary focus.

Many greenhouse professionals do make claims that the angles of roofs are clear and simple. Yet reality does tend to differ a little bit. So there is a bit more strategy involved, and here are things you really need to consider to get the best angle for your house.

There is a little formula called the angle of incidence. The reason why it is named such, and why it is so important, is because the angle of the glazing actually does affect the amount of light that manages to access the greenhouse. Consider shining a flashlight directly on a straight wall ahead of you. You can clearly see a concentrated amount of light has managed to land on it. The same could be said if you shone the flashlight directly through a window. However, if you were to shine the flashlight at an angled mirror or window, you may notice some of the light bouncing off, and the concentrated amount of light is certainly dimmer. The same can be said for the rays of the sun. If the sun's rays hit a window or glaze directly, one could say it absorbs 90% of the light. This is especially true if the glazing is single pane glass.

Considering the sun's rays do hit the earth at an angle, it only makes sense to build the roof at an angle too in order to make it as perpendicular as possible to the light.

However, this is where some misconceptions arise. A common pitch is an idea to create a formula by calculating the earth's latitude and just adding 20 degrees in order to calculate the slant of the roof. This does cause issues, however, considering that you will then have an extremely steep roof that is both impractical and could bring along several problems to sort out. The truth is, even if you make the roof slightly off by almost 45 degrees, it will not affect the light transmission too much. It just mustn't be too shallow; extending beyond 45 degrees perpendicular can cause problems and insufficient light transmission.

So, a good way to calculate your roof angle is by finding out the latitude and adding 20 degrees. This is your optimal angle. Then subtract it by 45 degrees to know how far you can alter it without losing a significant percentage of light. In the end, you can then work between the two numbers to build a roof both optimal for the light and practical for you, especially when it comes to the design. This is a practical and strategic way to approach building your roof. The math is not too complicated either.

Different Types of Foundations

The scariest thing to experience speeding on the highway is the encounter of an obstacle course of little bumps and tiny hills smashing against the tires of your vehicle. This is due to a lack of proper foundation and defeats the entire purpose of the road itself. Foundations for a greenhouse might not go as terribly wrong as foundations laid incorrectly on the road, but just like any building, it should be taken seriously. Unless, of course, your greenhouse is small enough not to have to build a foundation at all. Again this is entirely up to you.

You do need to consider these three factors when laying the foundation of your greenhouse: soil connection, the frost line, and your goals.

A greenhouse should have a connection with the soil. Anyone who has watched two plants growing side by side, one in a pot and one in the free ground, can always see a vast difference, where the one in the free soil flourishes bountifully, and the other has a constant struggle. This is because the roots are very limited in pots, whereas on free soil, the plants stretch out as far and as deep as need be.

In order to avoid troubles in winter, the soil does, for a start, need to be below the known frost line, and lastly, it should not be toxic. You can normally tell if the soil is contaminated by certain indications, such as soil discolorations. If there are particularly strong odors coming from the soil, then you may want to reconsider using it. If you also fail to see a lack of vegetation or plants struggling to grow there, it is a good indicator of whether or not the soil is toxic. You do need to consider the history of the area and the land you are in. If you are close to any mining, agriculture, gas dispensing, or even waste disposal, it could leave room for problems. If push comes to shove, you can have a certified laboratory test it, but that is up to you. You just want to make absolutely sure that the soil you use for your greenhouse is fresh and clean.

You also need to have your soil align with your goals, as not all soil is the same. Just like saltwater fish cannot survive in a lake nor freshwater fish in the ocean, the same can be said for the plants. Certain plants live and thrive in specific soil types, whereas others would simply shrivel up and die. As grim as that sounds, the truth remains very clear that you cannot plan your greenhouse under the belief that all plants will coexist and live peacefully in one place. You can consider grouping different plants together with the different soils, though, as this can open up the option of growing a variety of different plants despite their needs.

Foundation Insulation

The ground is a clever and practical way to start your insulation process. Yet you may be surprised at how many people forget or don't realize that they can use the same soil for the greenhouse to help with the heating. Foundation insulation is standard in greenhouses, but many people have started to adopt it for their own residential houses. So, why not add proper insulation for your greenhouse right underneath you? This will boost your overall insulation as well as cut out any necessary electricity costs. This certainly makes it self-sufficient in the long haul.

By insulating the greenhouse, you couple it with thermal

mass underground, which gradually releases its heat in the cool of the day and the evening, thus creating natural insulation and an evening out the temperature swings. Although there are many ways to make insulation, it is indeed best to focus on insulating underground. First, you create a soil pocket. This is a way to tap into a gold mine of free heat known as thermal mass (heat stored in the ground below). You may have heard or seen some people bury their greenhouses half underground. This is all to take advantage of the underground heat.

Here are three different types of foundations you can consider building for yourself. The first one directly tackles the issues pertaining to the frost. You can start off by creating shallow foundations and build-in insulated strips that stem along the wall. This does allow plants to have the freedom of expanding their roots while avoiding frost. However, this does place a limitation on the plants you can grow as some need deeper foundations depending on their root type.

You could consider the exact opposite and go for deep foundations where the plants can grow and thrive, and you do have fewer limitations. However, you will practically have to invest in digging deeper, laying down concrete insulated walls, and then only filling up with soil. This does solve the problems you may come across regarding frost, but it does mean you will have to budget accordingly. It will also take a little more time as the concrete will need time to cure.

Another option is to consider shooting for the rubble trench foundation. This is cheaper than the option above yet has been known to last long as well as work against the frost. However, this is not a vastly popular method, and many people are not actually aware of this type of foundation. So, if you intend on hiring someone to build a greenhouse for you, make sure they brush up on the necessary steps in order to create this successfully. The most significant benefit of this form is that little to practically no concrete is actually needed.

However, this may prod you to ask, is an insulated foundation really necessary? Well, truthfully, no. A person can make a passive solar greenhouse without it, but much like there are safety bars on the stairs and pipes for water in houses, it sure helps. Greenhouse foundations can lose approximately 15% of their heat just through the ground (Greenhouse Emporium, 2019). Therefore, in order to help with protecting your plant's roots and adding to your success with your greenhouse, you need to consider insulating it, especially if you want to avoid having to add any electrical assistance to the heating of your greenhouse as far as humanly possible.

You might wonder what a frost line is and how to know how deep to dig. A frost line is considered to be the depth where the ground happens to freeze in the winter. This means the soil on the very surface tends to freeze. However, the deeper you dig, the warmer it gets (due to natural thermal mass) to the point that the soil cannot freeze. This is important to know in a greenhouse, assuming you do not want your plant's roots to freeze and die. Therefore, it makes logical sense to dig below the frost line in order to prevent this from occurring.

A good tip is to consider waiting before digging the foundation if you are currently in the winter. Then, when summer arrives, the ground will be adequately thawed and just make your life overall easier when you are building and digging.

The best way to figure out your specific frost line is by checking out a frost line map. Much like figuring out the latitude and the angle you should build your greenhouse, there are maps to help you figure out the frost line. This does make the work infinitely more manageable as you do not have to be left at the mercy of trying to figure it out yourself. If you want better accuracy, you can check out your frost line using the National Weather Service's map or checking out your zip code.

Also, it is best to avoid any potential water pipes. If you are digging below the frost line, you will actually be reaching low enough actually to damage the water pipes. If you know the layout of your house, be sure not to dig your foundation right where the pipes are. If you are uncertain, then practice extra caution. Of course, a person wants to build their own passive solar greenhouse to save money and be self-sufficient inevitably, but it is best to play safe and avoid a visit from the local plumber as well.

All you really need to dig is a shovel, but you might want to have a pry bar handy if you happen to have large rocks in your area. Unfortunately, you may only discover this after you actually start digging. The fastest way to dig that will save both time and money is renting a handheld drill. You can even consider a Power Take-Off (PTO) tractor (in order to use more power to dig hard soil), and renting makes it significantly cheaper. You are making your life easier in the first steps of building the greenhouse, as it is potentially one of the longest and hardest steps when first starting off your greenhouse.

You will be learning about insulation a little more in-depth later in the next chapter. However, it is best now to understand the importance that a foundation holds. It is not merely to keep a building firm, steady, and upright (which is practically very important). Still, the insulation will help your passive solar greenhouse's journey to become self-sufficient. It isn't that difficult to lay yourself an insulated underground and save you a lot on the electricity bill in the long run and prevent death by frost for many of your plants.

If you happen to build a small passive greenhouse, then you could decide not to have a foundation at all. This is the fastest and most affordable option, but again, it is up to you. On the other hand, suppose you would like to have space and insulation, then a foundation is highly recommended. It all depends on your plans, budget, and goals for your solar passive greenhouse.

Chapter 4:
Insulation and Glazing

Having covered the insulation on the floor, a person can't help but wonder what other steps are to insulate the rest of the greenhouse. Avoiding heat loss is essential, especially in winter. You could wash a couple of weeks' worth of work down the drain just because of one extra frosty day and terrible insulation. This happens so quickly and so easily, so it is best to practice caution and good preparation.

Insulation is crucial for a passive solar greenhouse. You are considering that one actually wants to step away from using electricity, rather than relying on purely natural resources and clever sciences to make it practically self-function. Therefore you want to build smart. After all, work smart, not hard. It also means that you will be having a little bit of mercy on your electricity bill. You will find yourself and anyone else living with you thanking you.

Understanding R-Value

The first thing you need to understand about insulation is R-value. There is a lot of fuss going around about this, and you should especially pay attention to it. So what is R-value? This usually is a form or indication of the thermal resistance that is contained in certain materials. It gages how much an item can lose heat. Anyone who has gone down a metal slide would clearly remember not to wear shorts in the hot summer sun. The same could be said for a metal bench in winter. As quickly as it gains heat, it loses it. This has to be considered when you are building something to store heat and have it be released slowly, like a slow cooker.

R-value works in which the higher the R-value is, the better it is at keeping in the heat. This is very positive in regards to insulating your greenhouse. The thicker the materials are, the more effective they can be to put it as simply as possible. However, materials should also be low thermal conductivity. Otherwise, it loses heat just as quickly as it picks it up (like the example of metal chairs and swings). Or you learn to insulate those items to benefit from the quick transmission without the immediate loss.

So, you can consider R-value to be the key that measures the amount of heat your greenhouse needs and plays a role in the choice of your material. It is a handy tool to work on proper insulation, allowing your greenhouse to function optimally. It is known as the universal metric. You can consider using a formula such as:

Heat Loss = (1/R-value)(surface area)((ΔT) :(Storey, 2017)

There are certain ideas that clever spending on insulating surfaces that have low R-value will get you so much further than investing in items such as highly insulated walls. It is best to focus on the glazing materials, making sure it does have a good R-value.

Why should a person focus on glazing? Glazing is normally transparent or translucent material installed in a greenhouse in order to light in. If you have ever worn a hat on a cold misty day, then take it off. You immediately feel colder. This is because temperature escapes from your ears more than your arms at times. The same can be said for the glazing of a greenhouse. You can wrap it up as tightly as you want to around the rest of the house. However, if you forget the glazing, you will shoot yourself in the foot. Do keep in mind this is all in reference if you were in the Northern Hemisphere. If you are in the Southern hemisphere, then your solid insulated wall would have to be on the south side.

Your north, south, and west walls are also crucial to keep in mind while insulating, considering your passive solar greenhouse doesn't only focus on taking in the sun's energy but also storing it for the colder days and evenings.

The most common reason people fail with the construction of the greenhouse is due to the fact that they design it to capture heat perfectly. However, it slips out of the house as soon as the temperature does drop. Therefore, you need to add insulation on every part of the house that does not play a role in collecting heat and light. This means that you must entirely wrap your north wall in insulation and the east and west sidewalls, considering these sidewalls only get a minor amount of sunlight. Therefore they tend to be more guilty of losing heat than gaining it.

To get a good idea of how much insulation you need, observe other greenhouses if you can. But, again, keep in mind it really does depend on your climate and where you live. If you have rather extreme amounts of heat, you may slacken more on the insulation and focus on ventilation. Still, if you live in an area of cold and frequent winter snow, then you should consider giving your greenhouse the insulation blanket it deserves to keep your plants cozy. If you would like some additional advice about building your area, then consider contacting a nearby greenhouse designer. They can give you information about the climate's analysis, suggestions, and tips to get you started.

The best way to approach insulation is by calculating how much R-value you need. There is something known as interest diminishing return. It means that you can insulate as much as you want, but potentially some of that insulation will be rendered ineffective and take a bite out of your wallet. In practical terms, a person can play it easy and insulate everything they deem necessary, but in the end, it is like adding chocolate flakes to a chocolate bar; it just doesn't do much. So, for someone on a tight budget, here are a few things you can understand when working out the insulation you truly need.

According to Avis (2018c), you can calculate that approximately 58% of your heat is lost through the glazing. Another 11%, 15%, 10%, and 6% are lost through the footing, walls, and roof. So when you double the R-value in the walls, it might only be effective up to about 6%, which means it truly doesn't help as much as you would like it to.

It is commonly known that most heat loss occurs at night via glazing. So, a practical idea is applying a thermal curtain during the night for the glazing, dramatically cutting out heat loss to an estimated amount of 25%. Furthermore, it only costs a fraction of the amount when doubling the insulation on the rest of the walls. Again, however, depending on your climate, you need to cover the general basis and recommendations. Your climate plays a huge role in how you will be building your passive solar greenhouse. The thermal blind is not the only trick you can apply, however. You can also consider screens to trap the heat during the day, but your budget limitations may determine what you can get.

One of the cheapest methods of insulating your plants during the evening is by placing a layer of cover fabric directly over the plants. You can use two or even three layers, depending on how cold it gets. However, to prevent squashing, make sure you suspend the fabrics on hoops or canes. However, although this is the cheapest, it does require the most manual labor.

When you use thermal screens and blinds, these reduce the work as they are transparent, allowing the sun access during the day while cloaking and preventing heat from escaping at night. It would be best if you considered all these aspects, as well as whether or not the size of your greenhouse makes these ideas more feasible or not.

If it is exceptionally cold, then you might have to consider a greenhouse heater. This is not vastly expensive and a great solution, especially if the rest of your insulation is actually well built.

Taking a Deeper Look at Glazing

Glazing materials are equally important when it comes to insulation. As you are now aware, the glazing lets most of the heat escape, but it is as important in capturing it. If the plants do not get enough light, they will not flourish. They could potentially die. Glazing is important, but it has its fair share of downfalls.

Most people find polycarbonate to be the go-to choice, but you can consider going for a double-wall polycarbonate, which is by far cheaper and a good alternative to consider if your budget is tight. To make sure you do choose the correct material, you have to keep a couple of things in mind. First, you do want glazing with the highest potential R-value. However, it still needs to have the ability to let in light by 70% or, better yet, higher. So if you happen to have a high R-value glazing material at hand, but it transmits 60% or lower, then you really shouldn't consider it.

It would be best if you also made sure the glazing is strong enough to withstand the beatings your weather and climate can give. If you are in an area of heavy snowfall, make sure you can hold the load. If you have a lot of wind, make sure it can withstand those beatings too. Nothing will ruin your project faster than the reality that your glazing gets ripped off and your plants are destroyed.

It would help if you also keep your costs in mind. Buying the cheapest glazing material might turn out more expensive in the long run if it is in constant need of repairing or replacing.

This is often where the practical mindset of quality over quantity does trump this situation. You need to remember the amount of light the glazing can transmit, as that is the entire role of your glazing.

Now there is no magical fixed formula in working out the exact right amount of light transmission you need. It all does depend on the area you live in and whether there is a lot of shade surrounding your place. When you are in a really sunny climate, you can go for stronger glazing that transmits less light, but you may need more light transmission in the shadier areas. However, keep in mind the amount of light your glazing can transmit and the strength of the material work hand in hand. The denser forms of glazing tend to transmit less light, whereas the lighter material does transmit more.

It is always ideal for getting your material with a warranty, especially in regards to hail or accidental damage. This can save you a lot of sweat and tears should accidents occur.

There is also a difference between transparent and translucent material. For example, a mirror is known to be completely transparent, and you have no trouble looking through it. However, the glazing that is made of plastic is translucent, which means it is far harder to diffuse the light and isn't always necessarily see-through. It is known that translucent materials are, in general, better for growing plants, and it merely cuts out the nicer view you may receive from a transparent material.

Common Materials

Polycarbonate

Greenhouse Glazing Materials

You have probably heard of polycarbonate as it is the most popular material used to install glazing. It has multiple benefits, namely that it can withstand harsh weather well, is pretty hail resistant, and helps with insulation. It is also exceptionally lightweight and not such a massive burden to install. You can use it to seal the greenhouse professionally and can look quite aesthetically pleasing.

However, it has grown a reputation of going yellow due to all the exposure it may receive from the sun, but recently this drawback has been reduced. Polycarbonate can generally last a person for about ten to twenty years and is slightly more expensive than polyethylene film.

To top it all off, you can receive this form of glazing in a variety of layers depending on what suits your climate best. For example, you can get a standard double layer known to be about eight millimeters thick, or rather shoot for the five-layer, which is 32 millimeters and contains the R-value of 5.6. If they are both a little to the extreme, you can settle for a triple layer that is 16 millimeters and has an R-value of 2.4 (Ceres Greenhouse Solutions, 2017).

The most popular polycarbonate is one that tends to contain one or two layers. They are better on the budget but have fewer insulating aspects to them. This does decrease the efficiency of your passive solar greenhouse, and depending on your environment, you may have to opt for the higher insulating level to avoid spending any extra costs for electrical healing (as the whole point is to make the greenhouse passive and self-sufficient).

Polycarbonates tend to be built with certain air pockets. This creates multi-hollow walls. The air inside of these empty spaces helps to create a higher insulation factor. It is commonly called twin-walled panels and is quite common to use for greenhouses. Some even build triple-walled sheeting to add to the insulation. This is specifically if you are in a colder climate and could use all the help you can get, considering triple-walled sheeting has superior strength and an excellent form of heat retention. There are also thin-walled panels that do tend to offer benefits such as durability, decent insulating values, and light diffusion. You need to choose the layer and method depending on what would work best in your environment.

Tips for Installing Polycarbonate

When installing polycarbonate, there are a couple of things to take into consideration. First, improper installation can result in many drawbacks and reduce the lifespan of your glazing. Yet, they are easily avoidable.

Firstly, discoloration actually only occurs when the polycarbonate is installed upside down. This is because it is designed to have only one side that has a UV protection layer. If it is lying on the wrong side, it will turn yellow because the UV protection is on the wrong side, and the glazing will get damaged. Typically when the polycarbonate sheets are delivered, they have protective films with the correct labeling. It is best to keep the labeling on until after installation to prevent this mistake from occurring.

If moisture, dust, or debris enters the flutes, it is a guarantee that they will never look as nice as they did before. Unless, of course, you decide to blow out each and every flute, which is a painful chore and highly unlikely to happen. This is why you should store your polycarbonate in a nice dry place standing upward. Do not allow anyone to walk on it and seal off the open flutes with vent tape once you have had it installed.

The main concern for most people is leakage. Unfortunately, several mistakes allow this to happen and should be avoided. First, your roof does need to be on a slope of at least 10% in order to make sure all the water is moving. Second, do not allow any seams to run perpendicular to your plants, and make sure that any drill holes are larger than the screws, which will be acting as a sealant. This will give space for the contraction and expansion that may occur with the weather.

Acrylic

Acrylic is not like paints but rather a glazing that shares many similar aspects to polycarbonate. It is cheaper on the wallet and has common trade names, such as "Plexiglas." It comes in the same multi-walled form as its neighbor, and it's an excellent choice for applying it to your greenhouse roof and walls. This form of glazing can also be curved but has less resistance to impact than polycarbonate. It is more likely to shatter under heavy pressure, but it is still quite a strong material. Generally, if you have to decide between acrylic or polycarbonate, do what might turn out to be cheaper in your area. The odds of polycarbonate being more widely available is likely, but if you find acrylic to be the lower price, don't be too scared to use this form of glazing instead.

Created through shards of glass fiber embedded inside a form of plastic resin, it is commonly used for sports helmets and storage tanks. They have a wide variety of translucency and can most certainly be used to glaze your greenhouse. However, do keep in mind the level of light transmission is commonly lower, and it can be flammable, just like having a thatched roof. If you are in an area that struggles with fire occasionally or frequent lightning strikes, then you may have to reconsider. The reality is that most fiberglass greenhouses have indeed been replaced by polycarbonate, so although it is an option, opt for polycarbonate if you can.

ETFE

Ethylene tetrafluoroethylene (ETFE) is a new material that has many shared benefits of polycarbonate. It has good insulation levels as well as light transmission, and it is lightweight. It is known to have thicker material and can be curved if need be. It also has a longer lifespan and is resistant to hail. However, there are very few suppliers in regards to this material, and you should reconsider if you ever need to replace your glazing but just can't seem to find the stock again.

Other forms of glazing are known as film plastic that you can consider for glazing your solar-powered greenhouse. They are known to be low-cost, so if you have a lower budget, this might be what you can consider.

Polyethylene

This is a very popular, inexpensive material, but it does bring some disadvantages alongside it. It is not as long-lasting as polycarbonate and can easily suffer from the sun, snow, or wind. So, you might want to think things through if you tend to live in a harsher climate environment. It normally may only last you two to four years if it is in a very harsh climate. It has very little to almost no insulation, but it does provide a certain element of protection for your plants. It is best to use two layers and create an air gap in between to rectify this issue and create a certain amount of insulation. You could also use row covers as an alternative. In summary, this form of material is best used in climates known to be gentler. You will be doing yourself a huge disservice using this material when you are in an extremely cold and harsh environment.

Solawrap

Another option is using Solawrap. This is a higher quality of glazing you can use. It does have an average R-value of about 1.7 per inch of the material. However, in comparison to polycarbonate, it still contains lower levels of insulation. It is best for moderate environments and can last a little longer than its neighbor polyethylene. You can use this for curved greenhouses as well.

Glass

Glass brings its own fair share of advantages and cons as it is a different material in comparison to plastic. If you want to shoot something like this, you need to be aware that it is transparent rather than translucent. This does mean more light can enter and adds to the beautiful aesthetic of the greenhouse. It does have a variety of insulation ratings. Some can have higher R-values and are sealed very well, and are less likely to expand. This prevents any potential of air leaks which does have the habit of reducing the efficiency of insulation of the greenhouse. Glass glazings are also relatively affordable. They aren't cheap but still relatively moderate compared to other glazing materials you may have come across.

However, glass is heavy and can make installation a lot more complicated and difficult than other plastics. In addition, it does mean your overall framing will have to be boosted in order to support the weight of the glass, which may add to the additional costs.

Glass is by far more fragile than the other options listed and can, unfortunately, break with hail damage or heavy objects that happen to fall. This does add a level of impracticality when using them as roofs. In addition, you have to make sure the glass is tempered if your greenhouse does happen to require a building permit, which can make the glass far more expensive than you may have planned.

Tips on Installing a Glass Glazing

Rather focus on using glass strategically, such as for windows and perhaps the vertical applications whereas using stronger plastic materials for the roof instead.

A good safety tip is not to install annealed glass because if it breaks, the glass shatters, creating long and sharp shards. Stepping or being under it when the breaking occurs can really cause a lot of injuries. That is why it is best to have tempered glass, which, if it breaks, does so in very small square pieces. This minimizes the risk of injury to a significant effect.

Focusing on Insulation

In reality, glass can provide the highest solar light levels but still is not the best insulator, as it allows a lot of heat to escape during cooler temperatures. It is better to use glass that is multi-pane. However, this can turn out to be quite costly, and you may even have to consider custom ordering it for your specific sized greenhouse. This does mean that if it were to break, it might take a while longer to replace as well as be far more expensive,

If you really want to focus on insulation for your glazing at a more affordable price, then consider the twin-wall polycarbonate. It is easier to cut yourself and certainly has a higher R-value level compared to the glass. In addition, you do not necessarily have to stress having a reinforced frame due to its weight as it is lighter.

All in all, do consider getting curtains for your glazing as it does help to insulate during the evenings. If you have the budget, you can even focus on having automatically controlled ones, sparing you the pain of having to open and close them every day.

However, to make your solar passive greenhouse truly strategic, you can focus on balancing your glazing between both glass and plastic to tap into the benefits of both worlds. You can also be smart with the ventilation and the glazing by finding methods of storing the heat rather than pumping it out of the greenhouse during the day.

Focusing on Shading

Although glazing is meant to add light, sometimes a little shade is needed now and then and is a critical component. Especially if you intend to have sun-sensitive plants where they require shade from time to time. Although one of the main goals of the greenhouse is to get as much light in, there is again a flip side to this.

Shade usually is necessary if you are in hot and arid climatic conditions caused by direct sunshine. This commonly results in leaves that are scorched and bring along a host of pests such as red spider mites. Patchy ripening is also a common issue when it comes to too much sunlight. This can typically be the case for tomatoes as well as peppers.

There are three possible ways you can add shade to your greenhouse. First, good ventilation is needed as well as humidity. Then you can focus on shading in order to tone down the environment if need be. This typically adds to a more jungle-like effect for your plants, allowing many of them to grow without being barbecued during the course of the day. However, shading isn't necessarily complicated or expensive either, and your main goal should be to also reduce the internal temperatures.

You can add external shade netting. This is when you throw a large piece of plastic or hessian over the roof of your passive solar greenhouse. You can simply use clips to keep it in place and ensure the part is large enough to reach the floor.

This will allow you to comfortably secure the ends with bricks and not have it whipping back and forth as the laundry does on a windy day.

You can also consider using shade paint. It usually is quite easy to add to the glass as need be. It usually is quite resistant to a shower but might be a little bit more of a hassle to remove when the season does come to an end.

The last option is to consider internal shade netting. This is when you fix a plastic weave as tightly as possible in the very inside of your greenhouse. This happens to create a great solution without being outside facing the wear and tear of the weather. Again, normal clips used for the inside of frames are a clever and effective way of attaching them.

However, during winter, the shading is not likely to be necessary as you are far likely to be able to control the temperatures through ventilation. Shading tends to be for the extreme heat environments, just like the heaters are intended for the cold. It is an excellent solution for saving your plants and is quite affordable. What you choose, though, does again depend on the size of your greenhouse. If you have a greenhouse tower above you, trying to throw a shade net over it or even painting may just turn out to be very difficult. Instead, opt for the internal shading. However, if the greenhouse is small and space is too limited, then the paint or external shading might just turn out better.

Avoiding Common Glazing Mistakes

Yet again, it is time to learn from the mistakes of others and save yourself a lot of pain, frustrations, and difficulty. Even with glazing, there are quite a few mistakes that can be made and certainly should be avoided in the long run if possible.

Glazing Material

The most common mistake is making the wrong choice for your glazing material. If you choose glass in a severely hot climate, then you most certainly will be letting too much light and heat into your greenhouse. Choosing translucent or transparent glazing is all up to your local weather. It is best to purchase on the recommendations of your local greenhouse builder. There is certainly such a thing as too much light, and you need to consider it. However, if you do struggle with light in the winter, you can consider adding shading for the summer to save yourself some trouble.

Often, if a greenhouse's glazing is not built-in properly, it can bring in a glare. Anyone who has been in an office building or driving a vehicle knows exactly about this dreaded glare. Having to squint at your screen, or even finding the floor too bright, are common issues of glare that can cause eye fatigue and bring in too much light and heat for your greenhouse. Therefore, you have to consider the sun's position when building the structure of your greenhouse to avoid glare.

Glazing Set-Up

Yet overglazing is also a problem. It occurs when you add too much glass and have too little light entering your greenhouse. This creates the exact opposite of the desired effect and can again make it a less efficient environment for your plants to survive and thrive in.

Temperature & Location

You do need to take into consideration your temperature and location. Many of these mistakes are certainly avoidable if you are careful with your planning. However, don't be hasty, and give yourself the time and patience to wrinkle out any concerns and necessities. The moment you have finished building your greenhouse, you will find yourself an expert in many matters, including your local climate. All these things add up to some degree and effect for your greenhouse. As frustrating as it must be to have to work all these matters out, you are doing yourself a huge favor by planning in detail and planning well. Details matter, especially when it comes to glazing.

These matters depend on what you can afford and what benefits you want to take on. Glazing is an important factor in your greenhouse and should not be underestimated.

Chapter 5:
Ventilation

You can consider ventilation to be the flip side of insulation. You cannot have one with the other in a passive solar greenhouse. Because, just as you want to prevent your greenhouse from getting too cold, you also want to prevent it from getting too hot. Yet you don't want the ventilation to backfire against the insulation. They need to work hand in hand to create a passive environment where everything is working together as it should.

Importance of Passive Greenhouses

Consider this: if your greenhouse does not have proper ventilation, you will be opening a doorway of problems flooding your way. Ventilation happens to play four key parts in your greenhouse. First, they help with the regulation of all the temperatures, allowing your plants to get sufficient air and breath. Second, the air allows a plant to photosynthesize properly, which is exactly what you want and prevents the infestation of unwanted pests. Lastly, depending on the plants, it actually helps with self-pollination.

Common Problems of Underventilation

Temperature is important because plants can die from too much heat. Unless your plant is a cactus, it is best to assume they are sensitive and may end up wilt and die. Consider your climate, and if it has the tendency of getting very hot, then you need to focus on the ventilation.

You need to be wise in your decisions of where you build ventilation and how you build them, including the exhaust fans you want to use. The mistake that many people make is ventilating too well. In this event, the greenhouse does not trap the heat for the evening. Alternatively, the other extreme can happen, where it creates an oversized oven, killing the plants. It is great to find a nice balance in between to create for yourself an efficient and thriving greenhouse.

Passive vs. Active Ventilation

There are different forms of ventilation you do need to be aware of. You need to choose based on affordability, practicality, and obviously your own personal preference in what you believe will be best suited for your greenhouse.

Do be aware that even the best-designed greenhouse has the capability of overheating from time to time. This is because the very design of a passive solar greenhouse is to be a solar collector. So, although it is very much needed for the benefit of your plants, it can at times become a little bit like an oven.

You can consider implementing fans, which are known as active forms of ventilation, or try out the passive methods, which are normally solar-powered ventilators and windows that you can open yourself. The goal of ventilation is to give the air a path of least resistance in order to move. The best method to do this is by planting intake vents lower whereas placing the exhaust vents higher (considering the air lower to the ground is cooler whereas heated air tends to lift). This creates a passive method of airflow which is ideal for someone who wants to build a passive solar greenhouse.

If you want to get really accurate and clever, you can place the vents in line with the natural air movements in your local area. For example, if you normally have easterly winds, then it is ideal to place the intake vents to the east of your house and the exhaust on your west, or vice versa if you happen to have more common western wind.

Having control over your ventilation should be your main idea and goal. If it happens to be really cold, then it may not be the best time to expose your greenhouse to the frigid temperatures outside. The idea is to have the ability to have the ventilation at the right time and at the correct temperature. Many people have come up with a variety of solutions, and you can decide what you would like to implement in your greenhouse. There are three main categories under which they fall.

Manual Ventilation

The first one is manual ventilation. This is practically the simplest and easiest method of opening your doors and windows inside of a greenhouse. It may seem to be the cheapest method, but in reality, it may tally up some more costs. Manual ventilation does require everyday attention, much like a pet, and may even need to be opened or closed during certain times of the day. In addition, as the temperature fluctuates, your ventilation needs to change accordingly. This means you will be racking up a lot of trips to your greenhouse, and depending on where your greenhouse is, this could make it even more difficult.

Solar Vents

Your next option is solar vents. These are obviously powered on a solar basis and tend to open and close depending on the temperature inside your greenhouse. In addition, they tend to use wax cylinders, thus cutting off the need to use electricity and still making your greenhouse as passive as possible. However, they have the reputation of being finicky and sometimes require custom openings considering they may not necessarily fit into your precise design. Therefore, it is best to plan your ventilation alongside the structuring and framework of your greenhouse in the first place.

Another issue that may arise is the need to protect your vents from snow, or possibly, extreme winds when they open. If too much snow falls into the vents, it can actually cause a blockage and a breakage. Therefore, it is advised not to build your vents on the roof or any potential spot where snow could accumulate. The same could most certainly be said for the winds where the vents could be accidentally used for a sail and get damaged therein.

Keep in mind that most vents you purchase at the store will not be airtight. Therefore, it is up to you to make sure that the vent you put in is fully and properly sealed before it becomes one of the major heat loss factors in your greenhouse.

Mechanical Ventilation

Another form of ventilation is a mechanical system, which uses fans or other forms of mechanical devices. This allows the greenhouse to create proper circulation as well as a proper form of airflow. The best advantage to this is because you have a very high level of control over the ventilation of the greenhouse. In addition, this form of ventilation does not rely at all on natural elements of the wind or thermal buoyancy. You can also fully automate your greenhouse with this method.

Strategic Ventilation

There are certainly different places you can install your vents that are strategic and work alongside the natural habitat of your environment. Naturally, it would be ideal to have a passive form of ventilation, as it is the cheapest, but this does depend on your climate. Because you will be focusing on the effect of the wind and the buoyancy of temperature in order to create your passive ventilation system, you can take advantage of the wind outside the greenhouse in order to bring in the fresh air to your greenhouse. That is if your local area happens to have a lot of wind. Not every environment will have this advantage.

Example of Passive Ventilation

Thermal buoyancy also works on the reality that hot air rises as the cool air enters. This allows air movement to occur in a more natural way as well.

The best way to fully use this to your advantage is by placing the vents strategically around your greenhouse through roll-upsides, wall vents, and even roof vents. The vents on the walls and the roll-ups tend to allow the air into the greenhouse, whereas the roof vents allow the hot air to exit above.

Keep in mind, this can be strategic, but it can also cause problems if you intend to use the hot air for thermal mass, especially a climate battery. If you are in an area where you do not tend to use a climate battery but would rather focus on ventilation, then, by all means, go ahead. It is just a good rule of thumb to keep in mind when building your passive solar greenhouse.

The one drawback to passive ventilation is the reality that you will not have much if any, control over the ventilation that takes place. You can most certainly feel free to take advantage of the weather, but do not expect a perfect commercial timeline when all you happen to have is passive ventilation. It might end up not being sufficient, which can result in your plants suffering and paying the price.

This is why having an active cooling system is important. Creating an environment where an average wind speed between two or even three miles per hour is ideal and recommended. However, for a passive system, it will rarely reach this goal, and this is why you do want to have an active cooling system specifically designed for your greenhouse.

When it comes to an active cooling system, mechanical tools

such as evaporative coolers and fans are required in order to create the necessary and needed movement in the air. Fans are, however, sorely underestimated, but they are very effective as well as efficient. They tend to be overlooked or even forgotten, but any professional greenhouse builder can tell you all the benefits the fans bring to the table. Anyone who has a fan in a hot climate can tell you they bring along their own form of cooling.

It works because the walls pull the air in using a damp pad, which then gets distributed by the fans. As a result, the air is by far cooler and humid than it was outside, allowing for a more amicable environment on a hot summer day.

This does cost more money, however, and a certain amount of electricity too. This is why it may be better to install passive ventilation alongside an active one to work hand in hand and cut any extra costs. The days that work well for your passive system will shave off your electricity bill and still keep the greenhouse going on an efficient basis. It is known as blending your passive as well as your active ventilation together in order to grab the advantages of both, enjoying the benefits of both worlds while cutting down on the cons of others.

How Much Ventilation Is Needed?

Again, considering you are building yourself a custom greenhouse, there is no direct answer to this question. Rather just a few helpful tips and strategies to make sure you adapt it according to how you need it. In order to get a good idea of the number, consider contacting your local greenhouse designer, or you could try using some calculators online. A lot of these problems can truly be solved with a little math which can make things a little easier. Even if you are not a big fan of math, calculators are there for a reason as well.

Here are a few tips to help your journey along. First, be aware that if you use passive vents, the total area in which you can open in the greenhouse should be an estimated 20%-40% (Ceres Greenhouse Solutions, 2015a). Again, this number does depend on your climate. Naturally, if it is colder, it is better to opt for the 20%, whereas if you are in hotter weather, then you could consider the 35% or 40%. You also need to keep in mind the glazing and how much heat is being let into the greenhouse as well. If you happen to have shading, you might actually want to decrease the ventilation if it is quite cool already. All of these are factors you may need to take into consideration. This is why it is recommended time and again to speak to a professional greenhouse builder. Although you are fully capable of building this greenhouse completely on your own, there is no harm in finding out information from someone who builds greenhouses for a living. In fact, it is wise to ask for help every now and then. This gets you quite a couple of steps farther than those who just try to go for it completely on their own.

If you plan to use exhaust fans, then a good rule to keep is allowing the fan to provide a ratio of one to three air exchanges every hour. Even using Ground To Heat Transfer

(GAHT) can actually provide a similar system to this, so if you have installed a climate battery, you need to take it into consideration as well. They work partially as exhaust fans too and need to be added to the total amount of exhaust fans you would like to install. Therefore, if you do have a climate battery, it is recommended to then install smaller fans alongside them.

All in all, just like you would like to determine the amount of R-value to put into the greenhouse, it is all about working out the sum total of everything. This is where you might need to experiment with your plans, especially if you would like to combine your passive ventilation with mechanical.

Ventilation Volume Rates During The Seasons

There is normally an accepted rate of ventilation when the summer season heats (Garden & Greenhouse, 2012). This is about one air change per minute. How do people measure this? Well, fans are normally rated through the amount of air volume they actually move. This is usually used in the ratio of cubic feet per minute.

Naturally, it makes sense that you need to work out the total volume of your greenhouse in cubic feet. This is done by multiplying the length and width together alongside the height of your greenhouse. This will give you the measurements of your greenhouse's volume.

Keep in mind, the greenhouse's roof does happen to come at an angle. Thus your greenhouse is not a perfect rectangle, and it does mess a little with the math. It can make the calculations just a little bit more difficult. If the thought of math is scary, worry not; a degree in geometry is not actually required. Just a little brush up on some math you have learned in school (this is where people who ask where and how they solve X can actually help them until they decide to build something, say a greenhouse on their own). The easiest and simplest approach is by adding the average 10 ft height that is tacked and constant for the average greenhouse.

It may not be as entirely accurate as you had hoped, but it will still do the job. For example, so you know, the length of the greenhouse is about 50 ft, and the width is estimated to be about 20 ft. Then you can add the 10 ft constant height and multiply those numbers together is equal to 50 ft x 20 ft x 10 ft = 10,000 cubic feet (a calculator was used to work this sum out, do not be afraid to use one).

Now that you know your greenhouse is 10,000 cubic feet, then you would want to exchange and install fans that either have a rating of 10,000 cubic feet or get yourself another couple of fans to help the greenhouse out.

When winter comes, ventilation is needed at the minimum and almost never used to help with temperature control. During the fall and spring seasons, the volume requirements are bound to vary. There will be a balance of having to remove excess heat or add humidity, depending on the days. Consider autumn and spring are not as tightly bound to weather patterns as winter and summer are. This is where automated systems are proven to be more effective as they adapt to the day-to-day changes and environment. On a cold day, they focus on insulation, whereas on a hot day, they increase ventilation. It will be tough having to determine every single day yourself what the greenhouse needs to prioritize.

A good tip would be to consider oscillating fans. They are a handy tool used to create uniformity and great air movement. They also have the habit of extending the amicable conditions for longer periods of time. You could also consider using perforated polyethylene tubes to assist in the distribution of fresh air.

It would not be too far-fetched to claim that ventilation plays a role in something as simple as some of the plant functions, such as photosynthesis. It may also play a role in how the plants are pollinated, blooming flowers, and creating idealistic environments for you to grow whatever plants you truly desire. But, of course, it all hangs on the balance of planning ahead, and making sudden quick changes could hinder your success.

Common Questions Asked About Ventilation

As you start working on your greenhouse, you may come across a few questions about ventilation and find yourself a little stuck. Here are the most frequently asked questions about ventilation that should help your journey forward.

First, what does it mean to have a weather station? And why is it a good idea to have one? As well-built and designed as your greenhouse maybe, you do not want to be surprised by the weather. Weather stations are used to collect any and all info on the temperature, humidity, and even solar levels that surround your greenhouse. Some can even go as far as to measure the direction of the rain and the wind. You can install the weather station to work together with any automated systems indoors, which will allow your greenhouse to function with the proper knowledge necessary.

It is easy to underestimate the heat as well as the humidity as it is not something a person can measure with their eyes. You should consider installing a weather station where it is accessible. It does need regular maintenance and cleaning to keep accurate readings. This is especially important if you are surrounded by birdlife and leaves. It is best to purchase a higher quality system that will last you longer, as your data is really only as good as the sensor provided. Additionally, it would be working every day, and anyone knows that in itself is a major factor of wear and tear.

What Exactly Are Greenhouse Roof Vents?

Although it has been discussed, a lot of confusion could still arise about its roles and importance. Roof vents are cooling vents placed on the roof of the greenhouse that can be opened to release warm air. Cooling vents are by far one of the best methods to cool down your greenhouse. This is especially useful if you are in a very hot environment. The roof vents expel the hot air and pull in the cooler air from the ground.

Chapter 6:
Climate Control

Climate control fits the centerpiece of both ventilation and insulation. This is practically the knob you would use to create the reality of a thriving atmosphere for your plants. Having control of your temperature in your passive solar greenhouse is the biggest benefit. This is the fourth element you can implement in order to maximize the heat you gain in the winter and reduce it in the summer.

Understanding Your Climates

There are five main types of climates that exist on this earth. In total, there are many more than just five, but for the purposes of building a greenhouse, these five matter most. In order to plan the best strategy for your greenhouse, it is best to brush up on the climate that you are in and understand how the seasons in your region will go. Now you may have lived there for a few years, but people may actually be surprised how little they truly pay attention to the environment until it avidly affects them.

The climate is known to be the average condition of the weather that remains so over extended periods of time. This is known on average to be about 30 years or more. Even though the weather is altering every now and then, there are certain patterns that still remain the same. For example, winter comes at a certain time, and spring rises up afterward.

However, how hot your summers are and how cool your winters tend to be, changes from environment to environment. Some areas are certainly trapped in an eternal winter, such as Antarctica, while other places have an eternal summer, such as Tanzania in Africa.

The closer you are to the equator, the hotter most regions will be. This is because you are getting maximum exposure to the sun's light. Whereas, on the North and South poles, a person gets the least amount of sunlight. This leads to an average of being a couple of days in complete darkness at times, making it a little impractical to build a passive solar greenhouse there. However, these are examples of the most extreme situations, and most people are more exposed to average forms of winter and summer.

Using this information of the different climates, a German scientist, Wladimir Koppen, divided all the different climates of the world into various different categories, these are: tropical, dry, temperate, continental, and polar.

Tropical climates are known for their hot and humid areas and tend to have higher levels of heat along with excess amounts of rain. Building a greenhouse in this environment would certainly mean focusing on ventilation and less intake of light from time to time.

Dry climate zones, as the name implies, are known to be dry due to the rapid evaporation of any moisture. There is also very little rain that occurs and again more excessive heat. Ventilation for a greenhouse in this environment will certainly be crucial.

Temperate climates have the knack of being quite warm in the summer alongside thunderstorms and an average level of humidity. On the other hand, the winters are mild and tend to be less extreme. Again, for a greenhouse, one would add some insulation to help during the winter, but ventilation pulls out again as the first priority.

Continental climates are known for their mildly warm or cool forms of summers, but their winters are very cold. It is common to experience snowstorms and possibly strong winds in this environment. For a passive solar greenhouse, a person would have to focus on excessive light and higher levels of insulation. Ventilation will still be needed, but it is not the highest priority in this climate zone.

And finally, polar climates are known for their frigid, cold environments and are what people would describe as the eternal winter, as in summer, the temperature may not even rise above 10 degrees celsius. To build a greenhouse in this environment will focus heavily on insulation and light transmission with a little bit of ventilation to keep the airflow going. There is not much concern about a greenhouse overheating in this environment as the climate is devoid of most warmth.

Consider visiting the web and finding out exactly what your climate zone is and what your weather patterns are like. It is best to plan what you intend to prioritize before even starting to build your passive solar greenhouse.

Misting: Why You May Need It

It is best to understand that the sun releases infrared light through the greenhouse. A lot of this gets converted into thermal energy, which in turn converts to thermal radiation. The materials you use to build a greenhouse, however, are not able to transmit it, thus trapping it inside. This happens to create the ideal warm and humid environment that plants tend to thrive in. This is practically a nurturing area in which many plants can grow in your greenhouse but may not last a day outside of your greenhouse.

There are multiple greenhouses that close down because of the extreme heat. This occurs when a greenhouse is unable to maintain the passive cooler temperatures, even if they have ventilation. If you are in a climate that has extremely hot summers, then this is exactly why you should consider installing a greenhouse misting.

When installing it, you tend to help your greenhouse fend off certain diseases in plants, boost the growth rate of your plants and germination, and actually could be therapeutic to the plants (in simplest terms, the stress on plants reduces). With a misting system, you are more likely to maintain control of the humidity levels and help to ensure proper plant growth. If the humidity is too high, it can damage plants, but the same can most certainly be said if it is too low. Plants actually tend to stop growing if the level of your humidity drops below 30 degrees. So, when you install a mist system, it tends to be an easy solution to what may seem to be a big problem.

Another cool hack is that you can use greenhouse misting to apply the fertilizers. It basically allows you to spray it on a constant basis, letting the plants absorb it and use it to grow and thrive optimally. Installing it is quite easy and can help you have a level of control over your environment. From the light to the ventilation to the humidity, having control allows you to build the best environment for your specific plants.

Keep in mind that for about every 10 square feet of space in your greenhouse, you need to spend about one or two gallons of water every hour. Then, to work out the total amount of water, you can simply work out the number of nozzles multiplied by the rate of flow in a minute. Then finally, you can take a calculator (if you haven't picked one up already) and multiply that answer by the total minutes a person happens to have in a day. This is about 1440 minutes in a day.

You can additionally install extra devices to help regulate as well as properly keep maintenance over your greenhouse. Even having a timing system should help control both the frequency a well as the length of the sprays that may occur. This means it won't be up to you to spray every five minutes to every hour, but rather just set up an initial system in the first place.

You will need to decide what kind of nozzle you would like for your misting system. It could be brass or stainless steel as they are recommended due to their durability. There are also a few other items you may need to take into consideration.

You firstly need to focus on low-pressure systems. When you get yourself medium or even high pressure, it ends up being an extra and unnecessary expense. Focus on getting nozzles that perhaps have 1/2 inch of tubing.

Keep in mind that the smaller the nozzle is, the finer the mist will be. However, the finer the mist, the more likely it will be evaporating directly in the air before it even reaches the soil. This is actually a positive aspect, as you do not necessarily want everything around you to get wet. If you would prefer constantly damp soil, then go for a bigger nozzle. If you do find that everything gets a little too damp, then all you need to do is turn off the system just for a little while to allow things to dry. Considering that you are using the misting system in the summer heat, it is going to dry relatively quickly.

You also want to focus on devices that are actually anti-drip. If your nozzles are misting and you switch them off, then you may find some undesirable results with the dripping. This is why it is infinitely better to install anti-drip devices to prevent drips from occurring.

Do recall that a greenhouse misting system will be operating for hours to days on end. Therefore, make sure you purchase quality, durable materials.

Maximizing Light and Reducing Heat When Necessary

The design of a passive solar greenhouse relies on strategy. A strategy that should be used to fully maximize the light in the winter whereas reducing it in the summer. Again, it does depend on the climate you reside in. Some areas are known to be abundantly colder even in summer, whereas others need more focus on absorbing light even in summer. It is all up to you to determine things with your weather.

Keep in mind that the angle of the sun alters during the four seasons. Anyone who has windows facing the sun can confirm this. For example, during the course of winter, it is quite common that the light of the sun hits at a much lower angle than when it is summer. This obviously regulates the temperature and the seasons. Remember, though, the angles to which the sun strikes the surfaces also change depending on where you stay. These are all strategic calculations you will have to make.

If you have vertical southern surfaces, then you may want to focus on a higher, light-transmittance glazing. The best surface for that, as you may well know, is glass, which soaks in the highest amount of light and heat. However, insulation is sacrificed to a certain degree, but there are strategies you can undertake to combat this too. When you need to prioritize light and heat absorption, some things sometimes need to give way. You can focus on your thermal mass to regulate the heat during the evening and have a great strategic combination of both high-absorbing light and heat while having strong insulating factors with other tools and tricks. It all depends on your priorities, and keep in mind that while you may sacrifice one benefit, there should be another trick you can use to combat and bring some of it back. Again, keep in mind the angles as well. Do not be afraid to revisit a chapter in order to brush up on everything you need to know when designing your greenhouse.

When summertime strikes, you may end up with the exact opposite problem, depending on where you live. On average, most of the climates do give off too much light and certainly do not hold back on the heat. You get extra hours of daylight to top it all off, and you can consider light to be lower in demand for your greenhouse this time of year. This is where you want to focus on glazing that is more translucent and not transparent, such as polycarbonate that has twin layers.

Thermal Mass

As mentioned before, there are several ways you can focus on keeping your passive solar greenhouse cool during the summer and warmer during winter and evenings. There are multiple options available for you, such as concrete, rock, water, or water and glycol, all of which can store quite a large amount of heat in a confined space. There is actually an endless number of elements you can use for thermal mass, and you need to decide on affordability, as well as the level of thermal mass you would like to put in it. In order to help the whole process, you can use a calculator designed to work out the total amount of thermal mass you are recommended to get. It takes into consideration your weak point, AKA your glazing, as well as the material you would very much like to put in (like concrete or cob).

To simplify the idea, it is better to see more thermal mass

than less. Again, there comes the point where too much can really inhibit the production space of the greenhouse. It is very much like your insulation and ventilation; you need to discover a fine balance for yourself. Furthermore, the materials that you choose also bring along their own pros and cons. You have to be aware of them, especially if certain materials happen to be freezable while others are non-freezable.

Looking at non-solid materials first, they normally have the capability to freeze. So, for example, if you want to use water as your thermal mass, you have to keep in mind that it can freeze. This makes it a challenge, as the very point of it is to provide heat. However, it is a cheap option, thus holding to its appeal, and is still very capable of holding a high amount of thermal energy.

Using Water Barrels for a Solar Greenhouse

When a passive solar greenhouse is used for yearly plantations, it can go through all the extremes of that climate. The structure itself happens to absorb and collect excessive amounts of heat during the day, allowing a place to overheat quite easily. Yet if not built properly, it can easily lack insulation and freeze during the night. This is why people who own a greenhouse turn to a more stabilized form of maintaining the temperature by focusing on cooling the greenhouse during the day and heating it over the night. These strategies are known to be quite reliable yet costly as well. It is, furthermore, quite a chore to maintain the efforts you put in, and thermal mass is the solution to this problem. Nevertheless, they provide the best passive and natural solution to balance out the temperature spikes that may occur.

Water is the cheapest material and possibly the most popular one that is used for a greenhouse because it can retain the highest level of heat and is quite readily available. Every person would need a proper storage container because anyone could tell you that simply pouring it into the foundational soil of the greenhouse will get you nowhere fast (apart from hiking up your water bill, to say the least). Most people opt to use a storage container, which is quite easy to get a hold of and affordable as well.

The idea would be to stack a couple of large drums containing water into the greenhouse, creating a form of water wall that can be seen as the large thermal battery inside your passive solar greenhouse. One of the major drawbacks is that it can take up a large amount of space, which normally would have been able to be used for growing. So, you need to consider this option for the space you hope to have in your greenhouse. The smaller your greenhouse's natural design is, the more difficult this situation becomes.

If you would like to use a water wall, you will probably have to build a bigger greenhouse in the first place. Water walls tend to be used in greenhouses that are large or even commercial greenhouses. They are structured and designed to give the necessary space. You can consider stacking up the barrels against the insulated wall (whether north or south depending on where you live). Or you could consider using the barrels to actually elevate your plants. There are plenty of ways to use the advantages and bend the rules of your water wall if need be.

A good rule of thumb is to also ensure that your water barrels are in a darker color. Whether you purchase them that way or simply paint them is up to you. Dark colors tend to absorb and contain heat a little better than lighter colors. It's a small but useful detail to consider.

When using water barrels, it is harder to maintain temperature control. This is due to the fact that ventilation fans and heaters have settings to operate at specific temperatures, whereas water can be a little unpredictable from time to time. As much as anyone wishes they can control water, it is best to stick to science. This means water relies heavily on solar energy, and therefore this can become a problem if you suffer from really cloudy and cold weather on a more frequent basis. So, if you need another solution, you can consider using phase change material (PCM). This is a great alternative and will be covered later in this chapter.

Taking a Deeper Look at Your Water Barrels

Water barrels are ideal for someone who has a tight budget and faces severe temperature swings in their environment. It is a sustainable method in comparison to just insulation and ventilation, and it especially fits the theme of having a self-sufficient greenhouse.

However, you need to make sure you install the water wall

where it can be exposed to a certain amount of light in the winter and shaded in the summer. This is the ideal scenario but might not necessarily work out as such in your design. You can do this by having a partially insulated roof, and the water barrels are placed on the north side of the wall if you are in the northern hemisphere. If you are in the south, then naturally place the water barrels on your south wall.

In order to find the appropriate amount of insulation to fully understand or figure out when your water wall will have contact with light or shade, you can work out the solar angles. This is based on your location, and you can use a tool such as a sun chart program in order to create for yourself a diagram that plots the pathway of the sun. Then, you can consider using a protractor program and create an estimation of your roof length. It is best to ensure the place you put your wall will be shaded in the hot summer days and have a glimpse of the sun in the winter.

Phase Change Materials

The solid materials, known as phase change materials (PCM), on the other hand, do not have the high level of storage of thermal energy as water does. In fact, they have approximately four times less, but they do not freeze the same way water does and are far easier to set up without the need for further necessary maintenance overtime.

If you do desire to get a little more out of your greenhouse or prevent the need of having to dive in for repairs or replacement on your thermal mass, then you may want to consider phase change materials. PCM are used to absorb the energy of the sun during the day while releasing it at night, similar to water. PCM has the capability of keeping your greenhouse warm during the winter, especially the winter evenings. It is quite easy to add it to a greenhouse, even if it has already been designed and built-in, which allows a little bit more flexibility. For instance, if you do release the water walls that are not working, then switching or even adding phase change material is certainly an option.

How exactly does it work, though? Well, PCM works on the basis of the transference of energy, taking advantage of the natural changes that occur during a day. For example, a certain material changes in phase. It turns from solid into liquid and finally into gas that creates energy. This energy works as molecules that tend to combine and break apart from time to time. During the day, the PCM melts, taking in all the heat that comes through and solidifies at night. While it freezes, it releases the heat in the evening, passively warming up your greenhouse.

It is possible to use water in this form, but in reality, the PCM just works better. It takes in approximately five times the same amount of heat storage in comparison to water. The reason why is because it uses the physics of latent heat.

What is the physics of latent heat? Well, latent heat is known to be energy that has been absorbed and released through the use of a substance. This is when the substance's physical state changes from solid to liquid and gas. For example, when it is melting, the solid or liquid that is freezing is normally called the heat of fusion, and when it turns into a gas, it is known as the heat of evaporation.

A great example to use is that of a pot of water. While it is boiling, it is kept at the temperature of 100 degrees celsius. The temperature will remain so until everything has fully evaporated. This is because the evaporation that occurs is so large that it carries the thermal energy with it, releasing it once it condenses. This is ideal for creating thermal mass inside a solar-powered greenhouse. You will be using materials that change phases during the different temperatures.

So, phase change material, once installed, is practically free throughout the winter. It helps to even out all the swings of temperature evenly and creates an amicable environment for the plants. It is a very efficient energy source to be considered in your budget if you can since it focuses on the yearly aspect of the greenhouse and fewer concerns of it freezing over like water. Phase change materials, on average, have a better reaction to warmer temperatures than water, which freezes at 32 degrees Fahrenheit. However, with phase change material, it tends to be compatible for both hot and cold regions and seasons. All you need to do is tailor it according to the temperatures you are expecting.

Phasing change materials are quite easy to get a hold of, and it doesn't take a licensed person to install them. It tends to come in sheets that are nailed onto a wall for practicality. This reduces the space needed for thermal mass, such as water cans, and can literally be placed on any surface of the greenhouse. You can add as much as you believe is needed for the thermal mass, and it stays far out of your way, which is incredibly convenient if you have a small greenhouse. It is not too far-fetched to say that PCM is desirable for any passive solar greenhouses.

However, if you happen to be in cold and cloudy climates, where you cannot rely as heavily upon the sun, you may want to consider investing in a Ground to Air Heat Transfer or (GAHT). This is used to take advantage of the thermal mass in the underground soil, allowing it to store excess heat in the summer and slowly releasing it in winter. This means it works as an extended battery.

Climate Battery

Climate Battery, known as the GAHT system, is a clever thermal system using a couple of small fans. On an average day, a greenhouse absorbs a lot of heat, which is normally expelled through a ventilator, but this can truly be considered a waste. However, the climate battery focuses on drawing in any of the excess heat into the soil where it is stored and kept. A way of recycling the daylight heat, so to speak. The moment the greenhouse gets hot enough, there is a thermostat that switches on the pumps, moving the hot air into the soil. The moment the hot air reaches the soil, it is absorbed into the soil, and cooler, drier air tends to come back up into the greenhouse. This practically makes it work as a ventilation system at the same time.

When evening or even winter comes, it works the same way

to a certain degree. The fan, this time, draws in the cooler air, picking up the warmth in the soil and bringing the heat back into the passive solar greenhouse. This heat is the excess of what has actually been collected throughout the entirety of summer, not just the entirety of one single day. This makes it far more reliable with unpredictable weather and takes away a certain amount of dependence on the sun the whole time.

The tool kit of a GAHT system merely requires a couple of fans and a clever piping system that leads directly underground. It is taking simple sciences and using them fully to your advantage. Although it does make your greenhouse completely passive, it still saves you a lot of energy and electricity in comparison to other systems out there. Furthermore, some climates are so extreme that expecting your passive solar greenhouse to survive on its own is risky. Sometimes it just needs a small nudge here and there to help it along. Besides, it is still a self-heating system, as your greenhouse merely relies on the heat that has been stored in the soil, collected by the solar energy during the summer anyhow. It can certainly work in severe climates such as heavy snowfall and rain.

Another rule of thumb to remember is that the more humidity is in the air, the higher amounts of energy that can be stored. When the warm air is pumped into the soil, it condenses, which is the form of energy released into the soil. In order to make sure the whole system works properly, you have to make sure you have the correct duct sizes as well as correct sizes for fans. Otherwise, you do not use enough power, and the air does not actually reach the storage space. If this does happen, then you might as well have gone direct electrical heating elements instead. Because then you are practically storing nothing. This is quite a fatal mistake to make for your greenhouse, as by the time anyone might realize it is already winter, and no heat has been stored. So, it is better to ensure everything is done right from the start.

In order to make sure you build it correctly, you may want to use a SHGS design tool, a heavy-duty clamp, which allows a person to choose the diameters of the duct through the size of the fan. It is best to have a speed fan that can vary to improve the overall system. Also, it is best to install it as such so that you can change the fan speed and airflow rate that is optimal for your greenhouse, decreasing and increasing if need be.

Building Your Climate Battery: the Do's and the Don'ts

It is commonly said that it is wise to learn from your mistakes. However, one should call that knowledge and experience. It is wise when you learn from the mistakes of others before making costly ones of your own. So, when building your climate battery, there are a few things you may want to keep in mind, especially when it has cost others quite a penny and even failed in their greenhouse design. The very idea of learning all these tricks is to ensure your success, and what better way than to look at the mistakes commonly made by others and avoid them?

The idea behind a climate battery is simple, yet when it comes to the actual steps to building, it can turn out to be a lot trickier than expected. Here are a few do's and don'ts to keep in mind and elevate your success with this design.

You do need to create a proper plan at first, considering any small mistakes can actually make this design become useless and will frustrate you endlessly if it doesn't work. Most of the pitfalls when it comes to designing these climate batteries are avoidable, and this is where you really do need to pay attention. As mentioned above, one of the most common mistakes made is when the fans are too large or way too small. The way and amount of heat you manage to store all rely on the reality of how well and fast your air moves. You need to make sure that your heating, as well as your cooling capacity, is functioning at an equal rate. You have to make something that is powerful enough to push the airflow down, but if it is too powerful, the heat transfer doesn't occur. Rather, it simply rushes through the pipers and right back out again into the greenhouse, practically making the air go in pointless circles and defeating the entire purpose of the climate battery.

Another common mistake occurs when calculating the tubing diameter. They are designed to be too small or too large and should be calculated with the amount of airflow in them. If the pipe is too small, this will create a certain level of resistance and just a general reduction of heat storage and efficiency. Therefore, it is unlikely your climate battery will perform optimally and again possibly defeat the purpose of your design. If the pipes are too large, however, you end up losing a lot of the heat, thus reducing the heat and again the efficiency of your climate battery.

It is important to know how deep you should dig and place the pipes as well. Normally it is recommended to place the pipes around two to four feet below grade (Ceres Greenhouse Solutions, 2021). This allows the pipe to be deep but remain above the water table in the soil. If it happens to be buried in too shallow of a space, you are likely to lose the total store heat that you can use. It also works as a prevention of creating stable temperatures for the soil.

Furthermore, be aware of making the pipes either too short or way too long. There are multiple ways you can decide to connect as well as lay out your pipes in the soil. You can have it connected in multiple ways or even just have it connected in a single system. That is up to you and your greenhouse design. If the pipes happen to be too short, the time frame in which the hot air is transferred to the soil will not be enough. This will yet again reduce the efficiency of your climate battery. However, if the pipe is too long, the pump will struggle. You will end up reducing the airflow at a significant rate. This means it will store the heat nicely, but when the time comes for the airflow to pump back the heat, it will be sorely lacking.

Another common error you need to look out for is air leaks. This normally comes from improper sealing of pipes and again acts as a reduction of airflow. There is also drainage needed in the pipes in order to prevent or clean out the mold and potential blockages. Considering that it is warm, dark, and humid, it is an ideal breeding ground for mold and could cause many issues in your system if your pipes are stagnant.

It is also likely that your pipes could get blocked if you do not protect the entrances and the exits. Now a person certainly does want the water to enter the pipes, but dirt and bugs are a big no-no. So, consider covering your drain pipes with a thin layer of cloth and consider using chicken wire for your exhaust pipes, especially if they happen to be close to the soil.

Be aware that most greenhouse fans are not designed for excessively humid environments. Many people have tried to build inline fans that work on DC power which leads to a solar panel. Yet time and again, many of these fans happen to fail merely after using it for a year. Now that will be quite expensive to have to replace the whole time, and should rather be avoided.

It is also best to be strategic with the automation system of your climate battery. It is so easy to have it run moderately or even inefficiently. You can consider operating your climate battery on a thermostat or even a smart controller, depending on where you purchase your products from.

Now, here are a few things you should consider doing with your climate battery, starting off with balancing the diameter of your pipe in order to let it run at its best. When you balance them out well, you can influence the amount of airflow energy that is stored, and just the whole heating and cooling system in general. It is also recommended that you use tools and items carefully. Whatever you decide to get will have an influence on how easy it is to install as well as the durability. Quality over quantity often applies in this matter, but do your research as well. Just because it is expensive doesn't mean it is always going to last. Stick with reliable brands, and even consider asking others who have greenhouses on which materials they used to build their climate battery if they have one. Finally, make sure the parts you get are easy to access again. This is a practical strategy to apply, considering that if your component breaks, you can easily have it replaced. However, the parts you install should hopefully last for years, if not decades, even depending on the quality.

Another factor you might not have thought about is noise. Certain fans can create a low, constant humming sound, and if it is close to your house, it might just turn out to be a huge annoyance. Therefore, make sure to select fans that have a reputation of being quiet, especially if the greenhouse is close to where you reside. Again, this is a small detail that can make all the difference in the world.

Floors

Now, it is obvious that your greenhouse does not need finished flooring, such as what you would find in a residential house. However, most of the area will be used for plants and depending on the plants and foundation, you may just have to level the surface. There are three different types of floors you can use for your greenhouse to plan accordingly.

The first-floor option is soil. This is when your greenhouse does not technically have a floor, and you can use gravel, wooden planks, or even pavers if need be for some walkways.

The second-floor option is stone, gravel, or pavers. They tend to work well with raised beds considering a person does not want to have any flooring materials directly underneath the beds. The ideal scenario is to have insulated soil, in which the plants can spread their roots and thrive without suffering from frost either.

You can also consider using a concrete slab as your floor for your greenhouse. This has been a popular option, especially when you have a certain plan for your greenhouse. It brings alongside a number of benefits in comparison to the soil, gravel, or even stone. For instance, anything on wheels can easily be moved from place to place. It is not too far-fetched to bring and move a wheelbarrow, if at all necessary. It is certainly easier to keep clean and wash down. It can most certainly act as your foundation, and it is much easier to add a climate battery, as concrete not only creates an additional amount of thermal mass but also acts as a stabilizer. However, concrete can be quite costly, and you need to take this into consideration with your budget. A good idea is to get a quote from your local contractor in order to have a thorough understanding of how much it would cost you to install a concrete slab.

Keep in mind, a greenhouse is high in humidity, and anything contained inside should be humidity resistant, that includes the floor and multiple other items. The last thing you want is to have plant holders, tools, or even for the floor to rust or rot due to the natural humidity. Most people do not realize what water damage is. For a greenhouse, everything needs to be practically waterproof.

Importance of Drainage

Drainage plays a crucial role in your passive greenhouse, considering that if there is waterlogging, the damage can be quite serious. That is why it is recommended to build something called a French drain. If you have not heard of a French drain before, it is, in the simplest of terms, a drain pipe that is underground. The idea is to dig the pipe in at a certain angle. This prevents the surface area in your greenhouse from flooding and is possibly a good and affordable option to remove any waterlogged area in your greenhouse. The biggest advantage of it is its low price and simple design.

Building a drain pipe is not rocket science, and you do not necessarily need any special tools or massively complex equipment, but there are certain things you need to know and keep in mind.

The only thing you will need to figure out is where exactly you intend to dig the trench. Specifically, where the water will have direct access to. Keep in mind: you do not want to have the rainwater mix with the foul water drainage.

Foul drainage is water that is carrying properties, such as from washing machines, sinks, baths, and even toilets. When you mix the two up, you end up creating a high pollutant risk that is combined with very harmful chemicals. You can avoid this mistake by looking up the building regulations locally and checking out the planned drainage system.

So, how exactly do you install a French drain for your greenhouse? Firstly you start by digging two trenches. One could be the walking path in the middle of your greenhouse, and the other could be on the lower end of the wall right outside the greenhouse. It is best to keep your trench approximately three feet, or one meter, away from your building and make sure that the slope bottoms of your trench are facing downwards to a certain degree. It is recommended to have it drop about 0.25 per foot (M., 2018). You should also make sure the slope is pointed away from the greenhouse itself with about a minimum recommendation to have it at a 45 degrees angle. This creates the surety that all the soil that surrounds the trench is actually stable.

The next step would be to remain digging ditches at the end of the wall that is both in the greenhouse and outside. However, if you do happen to have a concrete slab as a foundation, that may be a little difficult for the inside, and some reconsideration will need to take place.

If you have dug the ditches at the end wall, you should eventually reach a time and point where the slope happens to drop off. This way, you can end the trenches at a slope and ratio of 1:50.

The third step would be to take your time lining any and all trenches with a drainage cloth, making sure it happens to cover all the sides and the bottom of the ditch completely. Then it is best to place a perforated drain pipe into your trench using couplings to connect all the necessary pieces. Make sure it is placed properly and cover it up with gravel. It should be completely covered, and you can finish it up by wrapping the gravel pipe. It would resemble a little bit of a hot dog, with the pipe being the sausage roll, the sauce being the gravel, and the cloth being the bread that covers the ditch. Afterward, finish your trench by covering the remaining layer with soil, and you will have a professional French drain that assists with the water.

Additional Heating

Now that you have fixed or set up a proper foundation as well as drainage, one can only wonder if there are any tips and tricks into adding any additional heating if needed. Additional heating is especially necessary if you live in a frigid environment, and the insulation alongside the thermal mass just might not be enough. These are common in polar climates, where you may struggle to collect enough solar energy.

When deciding to build a greenhouse, it is required to have a backup plan in regards to heat. How you are going to want to do it relies on a few factors, such as the options that exist, which you can use to heat up your greenhouse, and what is the absolute worst-case scenario when it comes to heating, as well as how much it may potentially cost you per year to have the heating. Having a backup plan takes away a little bit of the sole dependency you may have on the sun. Although solar is ideal, it can sometimes be unreliable for days to weeks, to the greenhouse's detriment.

When it comes to the options, you have a few. This includes using wood, a heat pump, natural gas, coal or oil, and perhaps even electricity. It is best to approach heating in a way that allows for maximum flexibility as well as staying as close to becoming a passive solar greenhouse as possible. It is important to have primary and backup heat sources. The greatest reason being is that if you were to leave your greenhouse for a couple of days (such as work or vacation), you would not want to have to be concerned about the temperature of the greenhouse. This is why it is good to have an automatic source that can turn on and off on its own while you are away. At the end of the day, while you are at home, you can use the cheapest forms of fuel, but when you decide to go away for a few days, then you do have a backup source that will kick in. This certainly works better than the alternative of having to get someone to babysit your greenhouse.

How exactly does this work? Consider that you have installed a wooden stove into your greenhouse that fuels on wood most of the time, but you have a natural gas heater installed as its backup if need be. Wood is certainly cheaper to get a hold of than gas and can burn for quite a while, but the gas can certainly be considered as the main backup source, as it doesn't need refueling on such a frequent basis. Building additional heating like this certainly takes the human factor into account. Most people need to go away from time to time and cannot be ever-present to attend to a greenhouse. Yet, at times, it seems to have the same realities of taking care of a dog. However, with a couple of backup plans, you will be reducing the amount of trouble hurdling your way.

Keep in mind that the backup system does tend to be a little colder than the optimal temperature, considering you are not always there to monitor it. For instance, you are using a wooden stove that allows the temperature to remain at 50 degrees Fahrenheit (10 celsius), but with your natural gas heater, it may only read about 40 degrees Fahrenheit (five celsius). Yet, if it works and keeps your plants healthy and happy, then there is no reason to be truly concerned. Plants typically have an ideal temperature range and will be okay with some mild variation caused by the backup system. If you can, work out the lowest temperature your greenhouse can reach that the plants will survive. This is done by calculating and figuring out the survivability of the plants.

Figuring Out Heat Loss in a Greenhouse

When figuring out the size of the heating that you need, the calculations can be quite complex and puzzling. More so, when you put in glazing, thermal mass, and other forms of building materials, all are contributing to the heat of the greenhouse. Therefore, the main principle is to gather enough information needed in order to properly calculate the surface area of your greenhouse as well as the glazing material that you have (the R-value) and the temperature you desire. Then you would need to take the average of the coldest temperature outdoors during wintertime. There are also two primary ways in which heat is lost; one is through conduction, and the other is through infiltration.

Most of the heat loss happens through conduction. This tends to happen on the surface of the greenhouse, and you can also add a small amount of convection and radiation.

Therefore according to Bartok (2019), you can work it out to this equation: conductive heat loss + SA x U x TD.

SA happens to be the calculation of the glazed surface—you want to work out the total amount that is in exposure to the cold. You can work it out by calculating the areas of the sidewalls, endwalls, and roof.

The U represents the heat transfer from the glazing. Now according to Bartok (2019), (Btu/hr-sq ft - degree F) is how you work it out, but normally the value of an average single layer polycarbonate is 1.15 and 0.7 when it is a double layer. So it is about 0.6 if you are using acrylic or a double wall polycarbonate.

TD stands for the temperature difference, which is the highest temperature on a winter night. A good temperature as the norm for inside a greenhouse is recommended to be about 70 degrees Fahrenheit, but you can always look up your local area.

When working out the heat loss from inflation, you can use the formula: 0.02 x V x C x TD Bartok, 2019.

The V tends to stand for the total volume of your greenhouse, which is worked out through the multiplication of the area of the floor to the average estimated height of your building.

The C works out to be the number of air changes that occur in an hour. When it is a new greenhouse, consider using 0.5-1, and for a greenhouse that has been repaired and kept in high quality should be around 1.5. If the greenhouse is in a very poor and sad state, then a person has to make that figure about 2-3. If you are in a very windy location, then you have to add another 10% or even 5% to your answer.

Td stands for the same value in the previous equation that had been discussed. This happens to be the maximum temperature inside the greenhouse.

When you add the two formulas together, then you will have the total heat loss. It may be quite tricky and quite a lot of math, but it all plays a part in the success of your greenhouse. When you install a heating system, you need to have the output of the heating system to be preferably equal or, better yet, greater than the total heat loss you have calculated. Therefore, it is better to consider installing two small units. This creates a higher level of safety as well as a better form of efficiency for your greenhouse.

Using this tool can help prepare you for the worst-case scenario. It is certainly handy and saves you any pain that might come if the worst actually does happen. After all, setting up a plan is setting yourself up for success. Whereas failing to plan is planning to fail. After you have worked out the heaters you need, then you will be able to work out the costs for the year quite easily, including fuel costs, and maybe add potential repairs if need be.

Integrating Your Design

The best part about custom designing your greenhouse is placing in elements that are unique and not commonly found in an average greenhouse to truly personalize your greenhouse. Yet working well and smart can allow for a smooth and successful integration of the different elements.

Defining Permaculture

A person can easily determine the needs, yields, and characteristics that are intrinsic to an element. The needs are practically the tools you use in order for something to work or survive. The yields or the products are the plants you get to grow in the greenhouse, and the intrinsic characteristics focus all on the different traits. For a passive solar greenhouse, it needs heat, insulation, and a certain amount of ventilation. Depending on your region, as well as the plants you want to grow, it will impact the characteristics you want in your passive solar greenhouse by the end of the day. All of these are parts of permaculture. You can use the same process of figuring out the parts of the elements in order to work out the best and most efficient way to infiltrate and build your greenhouse, specifically when it comes to heating.

To put it as simply as possible, everything that a person creates has certain needs and yields. For example, you cannot stack and organize paper neatly together without a folder or run a car without fuel. Your job for the passive solar greenhouse is to work out all these characteristics in order to build on the success of your own custom design.

You can consider designing as matchmaking. Find a part that needs another piece in order to play a certain role in your greenhouse. A person can break every single element down into practical needs for you to work out, specifically into needs and yields, which can be the first wise step into the design.

The elements that could be considered to be installed into a passive solar greenhouse could be a sauna, wood-fired hot tub, root cellar, or even solar dehydrator. So there is really no true limit to what you could add to your passive solar greenhouse.

Furthermore, if you intend to add your greenhouse to your home, you need to keep it in mind before the vapor and humidity. Yet this is not impossible. Rather, you can use items in your house such as stale air, exhaust from the heat recovery ventilator, or even the bathroom fans. Your house will get extra space in regards to the greenhouse as well as a "grocery" store of free food literally a door away.

At the end of the day, extra heating is important, especially if you are in a region that has frigid winters. A passive solar greenhouse is not too difficult, but it has some complicated moments. That is why it is better to take your time planning and customizing your greenhouse according to what it would suit best. Keep in mind all the characteristics and plan everything before you even start with the construction. You should make sure to add all the important elements of a greenhouse and then some. Don't forget to discuss with local greenhouse producers, as they will have a load of valuable advice specifically about the environment and materials. You will find how incredibly rewarding the journey is once everything has been set up and you have yourself a greenhouse and self-sustaining food. Now with a basic plan, understanding of the important elements, all that is left is to build it. Yet where to start? This is practically the part when you put everything you have truly learned into practice and consider working just a little outside the box.

Chapter 7:
Construction Steps

Now that you have the foundational knowledge, it is time to take the next big step and move into the actual DIY and planning. You know the primary aspects to focus on, but it is great to have a general idea of what you should do and the steps you need to take in order to succeed in building a passive solar greenhouse. We estimated that it can take about a month to build your greenhouse. Be aware, this is a guideline, and you can tweak it to your own time and tools if you need to.

Tools You Will Need

Basic construction tools are a must-have. These items are especially important for DIY, and if you are missing some of these tools, you may need to go shopping first:

- Screwdriver Set

- Tape Measure

- Toolbox

- Hammer

- Duct Tape

- Flashlight

- Set of Pliers

- Utility Knife

- Putty Knife

- Handsaw

- Adjustable Wrench

- Shovel

The next step would be to figure out the ingredients of your greenhouse itself. What materials are you going to use to build it with? What glazing are you going to use? Are you going to install ventilation systems?

Write down a list of all the tools and material you will need to start. Then, check to see what you already have and what you need. You might only need to buy some of the materials after all the excessive planning is done. So, both gathering your tools and the planning of your greenhouse do come hand in hand.

Common Materials

Every greenhouse is unique. Still, as a beginner, it can be hard to know where to start when shopping for materials. Therefore, this is a generalized list to get you going. But be aware, depending on your customizations, some materials may not be needed while others may have to be added to the list.

- Pillars or reinforcement: iron, aluminum, galvanized steel, wood

- Straps or beams: iron, galvanized steel, aluminum

- Arches: aluminum, galvanized steel
- In foundation, foundation bases, or supports: concrete
- Securing of the cover: galvanized wires, aluminum, or steel that has been galvanized
- Canals: aluminum or steel that has been galvanized
- Crop wire: aluminum, galvanized wire, steel

Covers:

- Plastic Film
- Rigid plastics
- Glass

Keep in mind these are the most common materials and perhaps would not cover everything according to what you want (depending on your customized and personal greenhouse), but it gives you a general idea of what you may need to get.

Budget Estimation

The budget depends on where you live and the cost of materials when you get them. However, according to *The Passive Solar Greenhouse* (n.d.), here are some of the cost estimations. Again, keep in mind, it will vary from where you come from and labor costs. On average, total material costs are normally about $8,150 Us dollars, or $7,000 dollars (this excludes solar fans, panels, cistern, spigot, and cistern foundation/pad).

Normally, if you are unskilled in construction, you may need some labor help, such as a carpenter and a skilled helper that can work part-time. However, if you are well equipped enough yourself or have friends to lend a hand, then labor costs will be cut out for the most part (excluding an electrician or any services that do require a licensed professional). So, labor costs could be about $6,150 or less. Of course, this also depends on your area.

The totals given are if you intend to build a high-quality greenhouse, but there is the possibility to build passive solar greenhouses that are significantly lower.

Steps to Your Solar Passive Greenhouse

Week One:

Step One: Goal Setting

Time to set your goals. The best way to turn your goals into a legitimate design is by asking yourself the primary question: which climate do you want to imitate?

Depending on the zone, you will have to focus on the different temperatures. A good method of calculating the material you will need to create the zone you want is by asking professionals such as a mechanical engineer or a local greenhouse designer. Otherwise, you can consider using tools such as the USDA Design Tool online for a fee. Unless you are a mechanical engineer of your own, you may need help working out how to build your customized climate for your passive greenhouse. So, take your time working it out, as it is a foundational step into building your greenhouse.

Step Two: Location

Now, you have to figure out the location of your site. It is an obvious step, as you need to now work out the best positioning for your greenhouse in order to absorb the highest amount of solar radiation if possible. Take your first week making all the calculations and blueprints as explained in the previous chapters.

Step Three: Determine the Shape

This works alongside step two. After you have found the location, it is best to work out your aspect ratio and determine the shape or possibly even cross-section of your greenhouse. All of these are quite flexible and certainly need to be customized to your specific needs, layout, and goals determined beforehand. This is why it is best to do all the planning and choices within the first week.

Step Four: Order Materials

Order the necessary, customized material needed to start, whether it is the pipes for the underground climate battery, or the concrete for the foundation, or even just the metal frames. It is now time to order and customize your material in order to get started on week two. Where you are and what materials are immediately available also determines the time frame in which this will be built.

Week Two:

Step Five: Foundation Beginnings

Now, it is time to build your foundation. Considering this is a very critical step, it can take a few days to even a week to accomplish (especially if you are pouring out concrete which needs a few days of rest afterward). You need to plan its layout as well as consider all the variations and steps you would want to implement. Do you want a climate battery? If so, then you may want to plan for the pipes, fans, and installation. If you want to have a concrete slab alongside it, then add that to the plan. Keep in mind that you want to make absolutely sure the foundation is below the frost line. If you do not do this, you could have your frames twisting, and if you have glass, it will shatter. This is beyond disastrous and can be avoided if you just dig a little deeper. If you intend to pour a concrete slab, then make it at least four inches deep. You also need to dig a trench that is below the frost line and then pour it into your concrete wall. Otherwise, it may not support the weight of the greenhouse.

Foundation for Solar Passive Greenhouse buildings

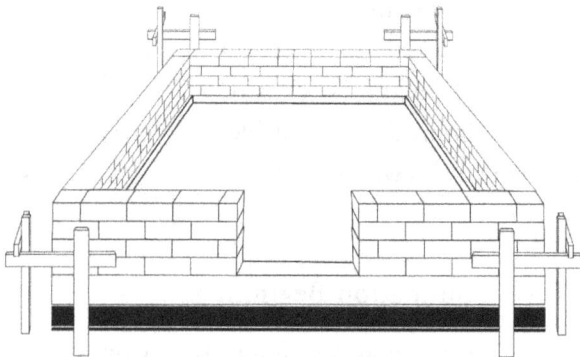

Be sure to rent any tools needed for digging. Even if you don't intend to build a climate battery, you may still have considered installing a French drain, and yet again, this involves laying a pipeline underground. So, be sure to have everything you planned ready when working on the foundation, as installing anything underground now is quite important and convenient before any form of the foundation has yet to be applied.

You could also build your greenhouse on an existing wooden deck, as long as the footings are placed below your frost line. You also need to check that the framing and posts are in good condition as well as resistant to rot since a greenhouse is all about humidity. The last thing you want is your greenhouse to crumble within a couple of months due to weak moldy wood.

Depending on your foundation, you will have a factor in a certain amount of time. If you start with no foundation, then the holes for the framework and the building are all that you need to be concerned about, and you can have it done within a day or two. Start off by measuring the footprint which your frame will occupy. If you do lay a foundation, it is best to plan this to be done in a week. Therefore, the next step-framing comes in week three.

Week Three:

Step Six: Greenhouse Framework

As you are laying your foundation, it is best to make your orders on the framework, making sure it is all customized and ready within the third week when you intend to start off.

Your plans of both ventilation and insulation should also be considered and will be installed along week three and week four.

Once you have prepared the space on the ground, as well as the foundation, it is now time to secure your frames to the base of your greenhouse. You will have to choose a certain style or frame that matches your foundation. This is a very important step for building your greenhouse, and it results in the functionality as well as efficiency of your entire project. This is why it is best to look up the different styles and frames beforehand in order to be completely sure of your decision, making sure it meets your budget. You will be placing the frames alongside the perimeter, bolting them down. If you need extra strength, you can secure steel cables in the X bracing shape to add to the security and strength against the wind and other external factors that might push the limit of your greenhouse. You want to make sure the foundation and the framework are sturdy from the start.

Greenhouse Frameworks

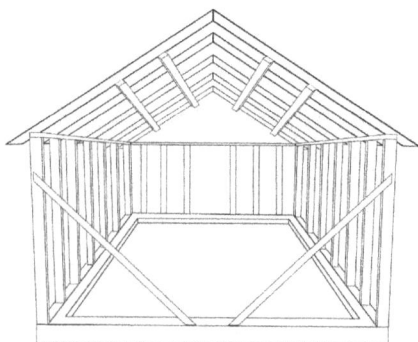

Once you have finished with the framework (the skeleton), it is time to double-check that everything is secured. This is inspecting the joints and all the connections. You want to look for any potentially harmful sharp points or rough spots that might harm the plastic sheet that goes over the frame. Using an angle grinder, you can smooth down any of these points. If you do not have the tool, then you could simply use soft fabric to wrap them instead. This will act as a cushion for the rest of your material.

Once you have the frame and structure set up, you will be focusing on your doors and hardware. You need to make sure you have both an entry and exit that works and fits with your greenhouse theme. There are a vast majority of door options and can also be insulated if you want to add to the R-value of your greenhouse. Make sure you get the proper nuts, bolts, and brackets to make it strong and have the ability to endure harsh storm conditions.

Your next step will be choosing your covering and applying. This is normally the glazing materials, as has been discussed before. There are a variety of materials available of various thicknesses and different R-values. Again, make sure you have a great understanding of how much light and insulation you want before installing it into your greenhouse. Finally, make sure everything is properly sealed. This can normally be done all within a week. Make sure any necessary appointments are also made within this week, such as with an electrician if need be as well as proper ventilation.

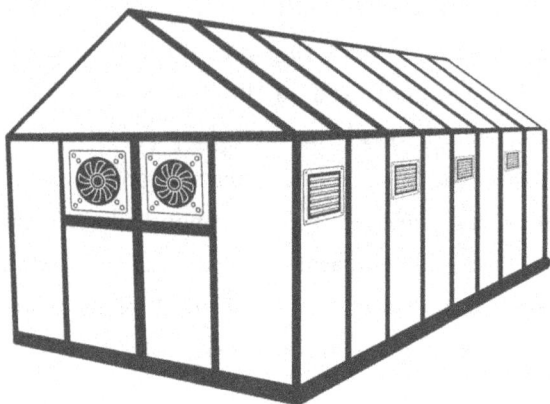

Week Four:

Your last week will be installing the last important parts of
your greenhouse, such as the glazing. Then, in week three,
the glazing needs to be ordered and customized according to
the frames that you installed. This might take some more
time, depending on the form of glazing you want. So, keep
in mind that this can take a week or even more if the
material you need is not immediately available.

Considering the covering makes or breaks your greenhouse
after the frame, you want to make absolutely sure it is
properly installed. The ideal installation would be that you
do not receive any wind or leaks into your greenhouse.
When applying your glazing, it is always recommended to
build on a double layer. If you install a single layer, you have
to do so at your own risk, especially if you are in a tougher
climate. You want to introduce an air bubble for extra

insulation, but strength is also important. Keep in mind, again, that glass always looks aesthetically pleasing, and plastic does eventually fade. If you do install glass, do yourself a massive favor and keep it insulated.

Step Seven: Installing the Glazing

Installing glazing is not too complicated as long as you make the frames square and level. Normally, a good kit will come with glazing tape as well as caulking and an aluminum barcap. This seals your glazing tightly, making it waterproof and far better insulated. Glazing tape works like putty because you will find it to be sticky on either side. You can start by unrolling your tape and pressing it tightly against the bars. Then you position your glazing and slowly but surely press it against the tape. Then you can use the butyl caulking on the edges of your glazing as well as installing the barcaps. The role of barcaps is to keep your glazing in place.

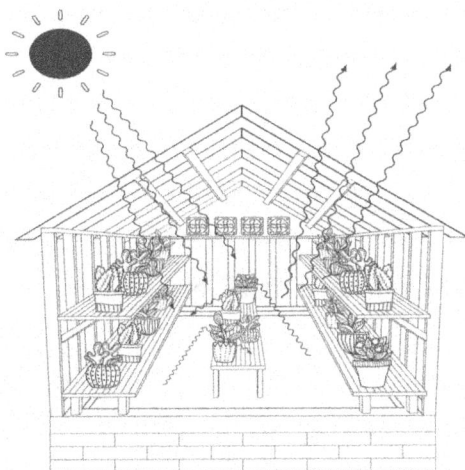

Step Eight: Installing the Ventilation and Heating

Your next step would be to place both the cooling as well as the ventilation. Then, you can decide to add shading to your greenhouse, passive ventilation, mechanical, or both. This can take a day or two to install, depending on the difficulty. You might also have to hire someone depending on the regulations of your country. So, remember to plan and bring in a licensed electrician when you need to install anything electrical.

Step Nine: Heating System

Once you have completed step eight, it is time to decide upon your heating system. After the ventilation, take your time installing the heating according to the plans you have selected prior, all customized for your greenhouse. Again, it is better to install two variations of heating. One with cheaper fuel and the other as a backup system, especially if you cannot afford to attend your greenhouse every day. It might seem easy at first, but the moment you are required to do it on a daily basis, you will not be able to go on vacation or go away for the weekend. You don't want your greenhouse to be your prison, so make sure you choose an appropriately sized heating system.

Step Ten: Environmental Controls

The next step will be to place your environmental controls such as thermostats or even computer modules and a misting system if need be. Make sure the items you install are user-friendly. It may not be all that necessary, and this is more of a luxury than a necessity, but when you install automated systems, it does create a more passive solar greenhouse with less labor work. However, again, it all depends on your budget and what you are indeed able to afford.

In Conclusion

Now that you have installed your foundation, insulation, ventilation, and temperature, as well as climate control, you are well on your way to a successful greenhouse. Feel free to add anything else you had in mind, including the containers for your plants or the gravel for your walkways if you have soil for your floor. You could consider a greenhouse bench, curtains for insulating your glazing, or even blanket cloths for your plants. Of course, all this depends on your budget and what you can afford at the end of the day. Now, you have a clear idea of the plan you need to formulate and the steps to constructing your greenhouse. It is not so complicated after all.

When building your first greenhouse, however, keep things as simple as possible, especially if it is your first time. The more complicated it gets, the more time you should give yourself to set things right. Of all the installations, the foundation may take you the most time, especially if you add concrete, considering that concrete needs time to cure. Yet if you give your greenhouse enough time and attention, then you will have it up and running in no time.

Maintenance of Your Greenhouse

Since you are planning on running your greenhouse

throughout the year, you will have to pay attention to maintenance after construction, as everything in the greenhouse can get dirty and attract other problems which just might come your way. Since soil is a major component in a greenhouse, it will get on everything and will sneak onto multiple surfaces and crevices. Whereas water evaporates, leaving condensation on glass or other surfaces. All of these can start to attract fungi as well as draw in unwanted pests.

The best way to maintain and keep your greenhouse clean is by jet-washing or power washing when your greenhouse is empty. Now, if you have pots, it is easy enough to move them outside as you quickly clear and clean your greenhouse. Or you can get someone to work with a disinfectant for you. When using a disinfectant, pick one that is harmless to the plants you are growing but tackles the unwanted mold and pests that come in from time to time.

You also need to be prepared for faulty equipment in the greenhouse, as materials do not last forever, and sometimes they are just poorly manufactured. It means, however, you need to keep a lookout for problems and fix them as quickly as possible before they negatively affect your plants. For example, when it comes to heaters, you need to watch out for corrosion. This is a huge indication of pipe leakage, and you want to fix it as soon as possible.

It would help if you also considered checking all the ventilation equipment such as doors, fans, and window seals every season. This is because many of them have the nasty knack of breaking down with wear and tear and abrupt changes in the weather. If you are using screens for your greenhouse, regularly check for tears and potential holes. The last thing you want is it coming apart on a bad day. It is best to keep them clear of dirt and any gunge that may build up from time to time with the fans. As you want to prevent breakages from blockages, and if you have a misting system, be sure to keep a lookout for leaks and cracks. This is normally trickier, considering that water moves away normally from the guilty spot.

If you have glass for glazing, then keep an eye out for any cracked or potential broken glass. If you find any, it is best to replace them as soon as you spot them. Considering these gaps can let pests inside, and if water freezes inside, it cracks it and makes things infinitely worse. Make sure to check the entirety of your greenhouse, especially after a bad storm. A good rule of thumb is to look for corrosion or potential breaks in the metal itself.

The places and spots in your greenhouse that you don't normally visit also need to be inspected. Making sure there are no cracks, leaks, or even signs of gnawing if you happen to have wires. Any system that may only be used on a seasonal basis should be checked regularly to see if it works, specifically any backup systems, such as your heaters.

The best way to prevent many of your problems is by adding a routine inspection into your schedule, once a week or a month. Make sure to create a suitable routine that works for you and your lifestyle and put it into practice. Just as you have built your greenhouse, you now have to maintain it, as nothing lasts forever, and accidents do happen. You want to stop a problem before it gets big, however, and this is why inspections are so very important to the overall efficiency of your passive solar-powered greenhouse.

Conclusion

Now you have come to the end of the line. Finally, you have the information and a plan to get you started in your solar passive greenhouse journey. This involves more than gardening, but you build yourself something better than a simple garden; you build a self-sustaining, eco-friendly environment for plants to thrive year-round. Building greenhouses should undoubtedly be encouraged worldwide, reducing the necessity of surviving on chemicalized foods and creating plant-friendly environments right at your back door. You may be a little overwhelmed by all the information, but there is no need to stress. Simply go back and review where necessary, building yourself a careful plan before going on ahead into construction. As the saying goes, slow but steady does win the race after all.

When building a passive solar greenhouse, you will need to remember the four key elements:

1. Orientation, as the placement of your greenhouse is fundamental.

2. Insulation is key to keeping your greenhouse warm and safe in the winter.

3. Ventilation works for reducing heat and adding humidity in the summer.

4. Temperature and climate control.

It may be drilled a couple of times, but they are the building blocks to a successful greenhouse. Sure, there are other elements you can add on, but in reality, without these four, your greenhouse is not likely to succeed.

Balance is also crucial because it is possible to have too much of something. There could be too much ventilation or too much light, or even too much insulation. Yet, the polar opposite can also be a problem. Working out your balance amongst these elements is moving ahead and thinking smart.

Yet, your budget may determine what you can and cannot afford or what your plans are. Keep in mind that, often, cheaper purchases lead to more work, which will negate any costs you would have saved upfront. You need to decide what you can manage on your busy schedule and even consider your plans for the year ahead. It is easy to commit from the start, but it is more a marathon than a sprint when it comes to a greenhouse and growing plants all year long. Keeping a greenhouse is practically like keeping a pet. You need to work out all the advantages, disadvantages, needs, and categories it falls under.

Furthermore, if you do not have the knowledge or are not entirely sure about questions and facts regarding your environment, do not be afraid to ask for help or information. You are bound to be surprised by the various tips and tricks people may show you. You could even consider joining online communities available on Facebook, as they are more open to answering questions as well as helping you out should you face any problems. Communities are there for a reason, and why not take advantage of the knowledge of people who have gone and built greenhouses before you? Specifically, reach out to those that have built In your area and climate and are accustomed to the limitations and requirements.

Be detailed with your planning and do your research on the items you need for your greenhouse. It is best to make your choices of the glazing, ventilation system, foundation, and multiple other criteria before even starting your construction, as many of the items need to be installed at the same time or at least prepared for them. Some things even need to be custom designed depending on your plans, and you need to adapt to that. Make sure the items you want are also easily obtainable.

Now that you are equipped with all the tools and knowledge, it is time to go out and use them to the best of your ability. Keep in mind to think a little out of the box and to customize the knowledge to your specific needs, location, goals, and intentions. For example, going for a passive solar greenhouse is shaving off a lot of money and creating a far better and self-sustaining environment than multiple other greenhouses built. Not only are you doing yourself a big favor, but you are genuinely participating in bettering the environment while providing for yourself your own food! If that is not incredibly exciting, then what is?

The journey ends here, and you have the necessary tools to proceed on your own. It may seem like a daunting journey, but this is a gratifying project that will not only benefit you, the community as a whole.

References

Arcadia GlassHouse. (n.d.). *Tip #11: Does My Greenhouse Need a Permit?* Arcadia GlassHouse. https://arcadiaglasshouse.com/greenhouse-tips/tip-11-greenhouse-need-permit/

Avis, R. (2018a, March 29). *How to Design a Passive Solar Greenhouse: Setting Goals, Site Selection, Aspect Ratio and Shape, —Part 1 of 4.* Medium. https://medium.com/@rob_74123/how-to-design-a-passive-solar-greenhouse-part-1-of-3-8c08ccbfbde8

Avis, R. (2018b, March 30). *How to Design a Passive Solar Greenhouse: Foundations, Kneewall, Ventilation & Glazing, — Part 2 of 4.* Medium. https://medium.com/@rob_74123/how-t0-design-a-passive-solar-greenhouse-part-2-of-4-e41471ab06e6

Avis, R. (2018c, March 31). *How to Design a Passive Solar Greenhouse: Light, Insulation and Subterranean Heating and Cooling, —Part 3 of 4.* Medium. https://medium.com/@rob_74123/how-to-design-a-passive-solar-greenhouse-light-insulation-and-subterranean-heating-and-cooling-7c66a27afd29

Barth, B. (2018, July 17). *DIY Misting System for Your Greenhouse, Barn, or Patio Party.* Modern Farmer. https://modernfarmer.com/2018/07/diy-misting-system-for-your-greenhouse-barn-or-patio-party/

Bartok, J. (2019, July 17). *Determining greenhouse heat loss.* Greenhouse Management. https://www.greenhousemag.com/article/technology-determining-greenhouse-heat-loss/

Bradford Research Center. (n.d.). *Passive Solar Greenhouse*. Bradford.missouri.edu; University of Missouri. https://bradford.missouri.edu/passive-solar-greenhouse/

Ceres Greenhouse Solutions. (2015a, January 21). *Solar Greenhouse Basics: Ventilation*. Ceres GS. https://ceresgs.com/solar-greenhouse-basics-ventilation/

Ceres Greenhouse Solutions. (2015b, February 24). *3 Types of Greenhouse Floors*. Ceres GS. https://ceresgs.com/3-types-of-greenhouse-floors/

Ceres Greenhouse Solutions. (2017, July 3). *How to Choose a Glazing Material for a Year Round Greenhouse*. Ceres GS. https://ceresgs.com/how-t0-choose-a-glazing-material-for-a-year-round-greenhouse/

Ceres Greenhouse Solutions. (2021, April 18). *10 Do's and Don'ts for Designing a Ground to Air Heat Transfer System*. Ceres GS. https://ceresgs.com/10-dos-and-donts-for-designing-a-ground-to-air-heat-transfer-system/

Claney, K. (2016, December 25). *Top 3 Problems When Installing Polygal (Multi-wall Polycarbonate)*. Regal Plastics Blog. https://www.regal-plastics.com/blog/top-3-problems-associated-with-improper-polygal-installation/

Garden & Greenhouse. (2012, June 5). *The Basics of Greenhouse Ventilation*. Garden & Greenhouse. https://www.gardenandgreenhouse.net/articles/greenhouse-articles/the-basics-of-greenhouse-venilation/

Greenhouse Emporium. (2019, April 8). *What You Need to Know About Greenhouse Insulation*. Greenhouse Emporium. https://greenhouseemporium.com/blogs/greenhouse-gardening/greenhouse-insulation/

Kosimov, S. (n.d.). *Central Asian Countries Initiative for Land Management*. Cacilm. http://www.cacilm.org/en/technologies/section/greenhouse/solar

M., A. (2018, March 1). *A Complete Guide to Greenhouse Drainage*. Greenhouse Growing. https://www.growingreenhouse.com/greenhouse-drainage/

Machnich, C. (2019, August 9). *How to Create the Ideal Ventilation System for Your Greenhouse*. Greenhouse Grower. https://www.greenhousegrower.com/technology/how-to-create-the-ideal-ventilation-system-for-your-greenhouse/

Meuse, J. (2018, September 11). *Constructing a Home Greenhouse*. FineGardening. https://www.finegardening.com/article/constructing-a-home-greenhouse

Mistcooling. (2015, December 25). *Why a Greenhouse Misting System is Worth Installing?* Mistcooling Blog. https://www.mistcooling.com/blog/why-a-greenhouse-misting-system-is-worth-installing/

Nelson, L. (2019, October 9). *7 Things to Know Before Building a Greenhouse*. Lawnstarter. https://www.lawnstarter.com/blog/landscaping/7-things-to-know-before-building-a-greenhouse/

Quinn, M. (2014, September 7). *How to Avoid the Most Common Greenhouse Mistakes*. Gardener's Path. https://gardenerspath.com/how-to/greenhouses-and-coldframes/avoid-common-greenhouse-mistakes/

Roe, B. (2017, January 31). *Greenhouse Misting: Creating the Best Environment*. Koolfog. https://koolfog.com/greenhouse-misting-creating-best-environment/

Schiller, L. (2016, November 29). *Climate Control and Your Year-Round Solar Greenhouse*. GreenBuilders Media. https://www.greenbuildermedia.com/blog/climate-control-and-your-year-round-solar-greenhouse#:~:text=The%20most%20common%20climate%20control

Scijinks. (n.d.). *What Are the Different Climate Types?* Scijinks.gov. https://scijinks.gov/climate-zones

Storey, A. (2017, September 12). *How to Decipher Heat Loss and Greenhouse R-Value*. Upstart University. https://university.upstartfarmers.com/blog/decipher-heat-loss-r-value-greenhouse#:~:text=And%20anyone%20who%20has%20begun

The Editors of Encyclopedia Britannica. (2019). Latent Heat. *Encyclopedia Britannica*. https://www.britannica.com/science/latent-heat

The Greenhouse Catalogue. (n.d.). *Greenhouse Kits and Greenhouse and Garden Supplies*. Greenhouse Catalogue. https://www.greenhousecatalog.com/greenhouse-ventilation

Thoma, M. (2020, July 25). *7 Useful Features You Need in a Passive Solar Greenhouse*. Healthy Fresh Homegrown. https://tranquilurbanhomestead.com/passive-solar-greenhouse/#insulate_the_north_wall

United States Department of Agriculture. (n.d.). *USDA Plant Hardiness Zone Map*. Plant Hardiness. https://planthardiness.ars.usda.gov/PHZMWeb/Maps.aspx

Image References

Aesthetic Greenhouse ninikvaratskhelia_. (2020, April 27). Greenhouse Flowers Blossom. Pixabay.com. https://pixabay.com/photos/greenhouse-flowers-blossom-bloom-5095328/

Best To Install Your Glazing In Even Squares/ Rectangular Structure La coccinelle. (2019, November 24). white metal stand in yard. Unsplash. https://unsplash.com/photos/ozXAKOBDkK4

Cold Climates Marek Okon. (2019, December 20). snow-covered trees beside body of water. Unsplash. https://unsplash.com/photos/ZNZ6EQscVw4

Common Example of a Kneewall Tiago Lopes. (2020, August 21). white and brown wooden house near green trees during daytime. Unsplash. https://unsplash.com/photos/45YovdnShwg

Example of Passive Ventilation www.zanda. photography. (2018, January 18). green watering can in green house. Unsplash. https://unsplash.com/photos/RBdE3jv5y68

Foundation Beginnings Blake, S. (2021, January 8). aerial view of gray concrete building. Unsplash. https://unsplash.com/photos/rsGd-rXFGkM

Greenhouse Framework Duncan, H. (2018, February 15). empty abandoned house at daytime. Unsplash. https://unsplash.com/photos/R4LfI6sygvw

Greenhouse With an Insulated Wall Harits Mustya Pratama. (2019, February 24). green vegetables. Unsplash. https://unsplash.com/photos/F47-qMQzVwQ

Greenhouse Glazing Materials Spratt, A. (2019, November 7). people inside greenhouse. Unsplash. https://unsplash.com/photos/YJGhQxiYWt8

Ventilation is Important inkanoack. (2014, July 14). Fan Fresh Air Greenhouse - Free photo on Pixabay. Pixabay.com. https://pixabay.com/photos/fan-fresh-air-greenhouse-technology-388937/

Off Grid Solar Power

*A Step-By-Step Guide to Make Your Own
Mobile 12 Volt Solar Power System For RV's,
Boats, Tiny Houses, Cars & Cabins Without
drowning in a Sea of Technical Jargon*

Small Footprint Press

Introduction

I'd put my money on the sun and solar energy.
What a source of power!

—*Thomas Edison*

Solar power has evolved to become an environmentally friendly, renewable source of energy and an affordable and cost-saving source of power. Its applications are endless, and improvements in the cost and efficiency of solar systems have skyrocketed over the past decade to the point where it is cheaper globally to produce power using solar arrays than using coal.

Our sun truly is the source of all life and energy on the planet, and we would be doing such a disservice to the environment if we didn't get more energy directly from this source. Solar power is reliable and predictable. You can easily track it based on the sun's intensity to the point where clouds passing and blocking out the sun will cause a noticeable drop in the energy produced by solar panels.

Solar systems are relatively straightforward to design and install. Of course, this is compared to other sources of energy, such as hydroelectric, natural gas, diesel, coal, wind, and geothermal energy. Most of these are far more complex, require far more capital and resources, and are not renewable. A common misunderstanding is that making use of a backup diesel generator is cheaper than using solar. This is only the case for people who think of the capital cost of buying the equipment. The actual cost of ownership for anything is in both the capital and operational costs. When considering this, you can see that, over the space of, say, five to ten years, using a diesel generator is more costly. You have to refuel it, replace filters and oil, and provide any other services required to keep it operational. You are also stuck with the noise that they make as well as the fumes that go everywhere. Hardly what you want for an off-grid solution. Compare this to a solar system which, once installed, essentially only needs to be cleaned. That's about it when it comes to regular maintenance. Every once in a while, you may have a damaged fuse, or you may be unfortunate enough to have lightning strike your panels, but these occasions are very few and far between.

Solar systems also have the benefit of battery backup systems. This takes out the argument that you can only have power when the sun is shining, far from it. When the sun is shining, you can make use of the energy and charge your batteries simultaneously, then make use of the energy stored at night just as though you were making use of the utility electricity supply. It really starts to look attractive when you look closer at your return of investment (ROI) on a solar system. This is essentially the time it takes for the solar system to save you the money equivalent to what you paid for the system in the first place. It is not uncommon for these systems to have an ROI period of around seven years. For a system that you could have in place for 25 years, paying it off over seven years and then actively saving money for the next 18 years is mind-boggling.

This is especially true for residential solar systems. When you start to look closely at your monthly electricity bill and see the figures drop due to your newly installed solar system, you will wonder why you didn't install your own solar system years ago!

We are Small Print Press, and we are committed to helping you sustainably survive and thrive while ensuring together that the world is a better place for future generations to come. Our mission is to empower people to mitigate all risks of potential disasters for themselves and their loved ones while still enjoying life and without living in fear. Having an off-grid solar power system in place is essential when dealing with natural disasters or becoming more self-sufficient.

Furthermore, it is only logical to make use of renewable energy moving forward. When it comes to things such as fossil fuels, coal, and natural gasses, we are limited by the quantity of these products that exist on the earth. You can compare it to engaging in a hunter and gatherer lifestyle versus a subsistence farming lifestyle. As much as you move from place to place, hunting contributes to the desolation of food resources in each region you travel through. These resources will never be able to supplement their reserves based on how quickly we consume them. Ancient populations started ballooning, and the hunter and gatherer lifestyle stopped making sense. Raising animals and crops in a set location made more sense for feeding the population. Over time, people could continue to grow more crops and raise more domesticated animals to feed expanding populations. Relying on a dwindling wild animal population made less and less sense. Renewable energy makes sense because we are reducing our reliance on finite resources that are dwindling just as wild game would dwindle with an expanding hunter population.

We at Small Footprint Press are fully aware of the detrimental impact we are having on the environment. We are consuming resources that have an expiration date without a concrete plan to address this problem. Moreover, we are burning fossil fuels to support our lifestyles and expanding global population while having unequivocal evidence that this behavior affects our climate and results in weather conditions that have significant consequences for our longevity on this planet. We want to create a lifestyle that is not destructive to our own lives and the ecosystems on this planet. It's often easy to forget that the tens of thousands of other species that live in this world have been here since long before we came around. These diverse animals, plants, fungi, birds, reptiles, bacteria, and everything in between all live on earth with us. We are still animals, just the same as they are. The only thing separating us is our intellect and recognition of others as individuals with their own conscience and thinking capability. We cannot continue on the path we are walking down because it will push us into a mass extinction event, which some already proclaim that we are in. This will escalate until all living things as we know them will die or change, and, most importantly, we will die off as well. However, the world will continue on. Life will continue on. We need to look past our greed to ensure our survival and longevity on earth.

It's not all gloom and doom, as we have been given the opportunity to make a change in our lifestyle. Although it may seem like a drop in the ocean to change your personal energy usage, if millions of people share the same mentality, then the power is with us. We are one with this world and need it to thrive for us to thrive. Our impact on the environment is unquestionable when looking at all evidence provided by science. We need to be more responsible and conscious. If we change by accelerating the transition to sustainable living and generating our own renewable energy for consumption, we are taking a step in the right direction.

Don't be disheartened by people telling you that the raw materials for solar systems require fossil fuels and that it negates its impact on the global climate, as these claims have been clearly debunked. It has been conclusively proven that solar panels themselves, made up of silicon, glass, copper, and aluminum, require at most two years of operation to generate as much power as was required to produce them (Svarc, 2019). The same can be said for lithium-ion batteries, which is a hot topic of discussion. Arguments arise from the mining of lithium, which is less labor and energy-intensive than the mining of aluminum. For the most part, lithium is a byproduct of other processes, such as brines, which account for half of all lithium produced from manufacturers. This means that the energy required to produce lithium-ion batteries could be provided using power generated by lithium-ion batteries, and it would still be productive energy. Essentially, it is an energy positive product, meaning that more energy can be generated from its extraction from the earth than would be consumed by extracting it (Talens Peiró et al., 2013). If you are ever confronted by people who argue that your solar system is more harmful to the environment than it benefits it, be sure to offer them these scientifically proven facts.

This book will go over all of the concepts around solar systems and how you can install your own. It will cover the basic overview of what solar power is, how you can design an effective solar system, and help you choose from all the different products out there in the market. You will be taken through some concepts around electricity so that, even if you have no knowledge in this field, you will be capable of installing your own solar system. We want to highlight now, and will do so again consistently in this book, the importance of safety whenever working with electricity. It is still very dangerous at the end of the day, so you must take the correct precautions, wear personal protective equipment (PPE), and follow the best practices. PPE consists of clothing designed to protect you. When installing and testing your solar system, insulated gloves and safety boots are the most important items to protect yourself from injury.

It is also important to inform you that there are laws and standards around using solar systems, particularly when you are interconnected with your electricity supplier. This book will cover some of the basics, but they vary from state to state and country to country. They are in place for a reason, and it isn't difficult to ensure that you comply with them and work with them to make sure that you have the best system possible.

If, on the other hand, you are installing a completely off-grid solution, then you only need to follow standards and safety precautions for your own benefit and don't necessarily need to register with your electricity supplier. It is a positive thing to see various laws and standards being processed by electricity suppliers because it shows that they support consumers making use of solar as much as possible. This book will focus on the small-scale, off-grid solar systems that you can install yourself. The primary focus areas will be in Recreational Vehicles (RV's), cabins, tiny homes, cars, boats, and other residential areas, such as larger homes. There are many similarities in how the systems work. The main difference is in the physical scale, installation procedures, and specific products necessary for particular applications, such as water-tight units for boat applications.

In the twenty-first century, there is a renewed drive for people to become more self-reliant and sustainable. You can reduce your carbon footprint, help the environment, save money, reduce your risk of calamities and generate your own clean energy to use however you choose. The only thing it requires is time, energy, and initial capital cost. Other than that, there is absolutely nothing to lose in installing your very own solar system. By the end of this book, you will be fully equipped to do it yourself!

Chapter 1:
Solar Power Explained

In this chapter, we will cover the concepts behind solar power and how it is possible to capture solar energy. We will discuss the terminology that you can expect to come across and the various components that make up a solar-powered installation. Don't get disheartened if it seems like a lot to take in. Over time, you will realize that solar systems are straightforward and not overly complex. This makes it the perfect DIY project to pursue.

This chapter should give you a good background on how to go about designing, installing, and testing a solar system, as well as the basics of what it entails. It isn't an overload of information and lets you know what you are getting into when installing your own solar system. In the following chapters, we will expand more on concepts, theories, and how the various components work and are integrated with one another.

What is Solar Power and How Does it Work?

Lying at the center of our solar system is a gigantic, burning fusion reactor: the sun. Every second of every day, hydrogen is converted into helium on a massive scale, releasing heat, light, and energy. The light the sun releases arrives on earth in the form of photons. Each photon carries energy, and solar power is our way of harnessing that energy (Marsh, 2019). Solar power is harvested from what is known as solar irradiance. This essentially means that the more intense the sunlight is, the more energy it carries with it. This means that you can harness more energy per solar panel in light-intense areas.

It is interesting to note that humans are not the first species to harness the energy from the sun. Most plants use photosynthesis to convert carbon dioxide and water into carbohydrates with energy from the sun. It is a process necessary for life as we know it on the planet. The earliest form of humans using energy from the sun was to light fires using a magnifying method well over one and a half millennia ago. This has changed a great deal over the years, and solar energy now makes up an estimated 2% of the world's total energy usage (Ritchie & Roser, 2020). There are countless opportunities to elevate this quantity over the next decade as the world moves toward using more green energy and less energy generated from fossil fuels. The efficiency of converting energy from the sun into useful energy is not very high based on today's technology. This is not a cause of major concern, as even plants have a very low efficiency of using sunlight in the process of photosynthesis. As technology improves, our ability to absorb more energy will inevitably improve. The sun has been providing us with energy for billions of years. As humans, improving our ability to harness the sun is a testament to our initiative to seek out energy resources that will not run out or do major harm to our environment or communities living here.

The natural phenomena on earth are the main driving force behind generating more sustainable forms of electricity. We do need to consider the effects of drawing energy from natural forces such as hydroelectric power, as this may result in water channels being cut off when building dam walls. But, in cases such as wind power, tidal power from wave action in coastal areas, solar power, and geothermal energy, we are not impacting the environment in any measurable way. The wind will continue to blow in its course and have the same impact on the biosphere as we know it. Tides will continue to flow, and waves will continue to crash in coastal areas whether we harness this power or not. Geothermal heat will continue to be generated due to tectonic motion and pressure built up in the earth's crust, making use of this heat not harming the environment. The same goes for solar energy, which will strike the earth the same way it always has. The primary area of concern with any of these technologies is the energy required to get the raw materials necessary for the products that harness this energy.

Although there are areas of concern, such as inhumane working conditions for mine workers in many developing countries globally, most companies providing the raw materials have a strict ethical policy that seeks to improve and uplift communities surrounding mining areas. There are bad apples and those who will take advantage of communities or individuals, which is why transparency in major mining companies is required. We should never stop pressing these corporations to ensure that they can source raw materials such as copper, lithium, aluminum, and other raw materials ethically. These activities not doing more damage to the environment is just as important as the benefit gained in using them. If it uses more energy to extract lithium from the earth, then why would we use it in batteries as an energy storage method? It wouldn't make sense to burn more fossil fuels in extracting the products needed. All major manufacturers are aware of this, and it would make their product non-profitable, so scientific research is always ongoing to ensure that the direction we are moving in makes sense. There is no scientific evidence that extracting required raw materials outweighs the energy-saving capability of these products, so be sure not to alter your perception based on people who do not have any factual basis for their claims. The age of misinformation is upon us, and the only way to educate ourselves is to do our own research, look at the evidence and facts that are proven, and push to get answers in areas that we aren't certain about.

How Can You Harness Solar Power?

There are two ways in which we are able to generate electricity using energy from the sun. Thermal capturing is used far less for small-scale power generation and is only used in large-scale power generation plants. From the word thermal, you should recognize that this is a form of

160

generating energy from the heat that is provided by the sun. There are also passive ways in which you can use this energy.

Solar thermal capturing is typically split into three categories: low, mid and high temperature. Low-temperature capturing is typically used in heating and cooling, mostly in buildings and living spaces. It is passive, and an example is letting natural light into your house for warmth in the winter and blocking the sun to keep a cool inside temperature during summer. The second form of solar thermal capturing is in mid temperatures. An example of this would be in using solar geysers. Heat is captured in collectors, and the heat energy is transferred to water in the geyser itself. It is a self-circulating system and a massive cost saver compared to geysers using electrical or gas elements. Finally, there are high-temperature solar thermal capturing systems. An example of this system would be concentrated solar plants that reflect sunlight using an array of reflector panels and focus it on tubes containing a fluid that absorbs thermal energy efficiently. The high amount of concentrated sunlight provides a large amount of heat absorbed by the fluid and used to turn water into steam and drive a turbine.

The other method of converting energy from the sun into electricity is using the photovoltaic process. The type of solar systems that we will focus on in this book are solar panels that make use of this process. All small-scale solar systems that generate electricity for homes, cabins, RV's, boats, and other vehicles use these solar panels. This is why many solar systems are referred to as photovoltaic (PV) arrays. It's helpful to understand this jargon and recognize why it is used. An array is a description of several panels mounted together to generate power.

How Do Solar Panels Convert Solar Energy into Usable Electricity?

There are two predominant ways in which energy from the sun can be harnessed to produce energy that is beneficial to us. The first of these methods, as I briefly discussed above, involves solar thermal energy capturing. Common procedures used to provide a function from this form of energy harvesting are solar geysers and solar concentrate plants. Solar geysers are mounted in order to absorb heat from the sun and used to circulate and heat water for usage, saving the electricity from using standard electrical and gas geysers, which require burning gas to heat water for cleaning, showering, and other practical purposes (Hutchison & Galiardi, 2019).

Another larger-scale example of making use of the thermal energy from the sun is concentrated in a solar plant. In these systems, hundreds of solar panels face a central tower, and this focused beam of light is used to superheat a solution that has been designed to retain heat very well.

A final form of this energy is in parabolic solar power plants. In these systems, solar panels are mounted in a c-shape, or parabola. These panels have a central line with water inside that is mounted at the focus point of the solar panels. The heat energy from the sun is focused on this central line, which typically carries water or another liquid that absorbs heat efficiently and can be superheated. The heat is then transferred to generate power. These systems are cheaper, as no cells are needed, only reflectors. They also have the advantage of not having a dependency on temperature and have a much longer lifespan than standard solar panels. However, they are far less energy efficient, still require cleaning, and take up a lot of physical space.

The other form of solar generation is the photovoltaic process. This is the process that typical solar systems use. When sunlight strikes the solar cells, typically made up of a semiconductive material such as silicon, it dislodges the semiconductor's electrons. These electrons are set in motion and flow to an area with a more positive charge. This is because electrons carry a negative charge and move to an area with a more positive charge via attraction. Likewise, the location where the electron starts becomes more negatively charged, this repels the electron away. In other words, a potential difference is set up between the electron's existing position and a more positive location, which results in the electrons moving and creating a flow of current. When the cells are connected in series, the potential difference across the cells increases while the flow of current through each cell remains the same. This boosts the power and is the reason why typical solar panels are the size that they are. They are small enough to be handled by a single person, easily replaceable, and robust enough in their manufacturing. They are also large enough to have each panel generate a significant amount of power. It would be more costly to build solar panels that are the size of a single cell, as more materials would be needed to build frames, increasing the cost of each unit significantly.

Off-grid vs. On-Grid (aka Grid-Tied) Solar Energy

There are two main types of solar arrays: off-grid and on-grid solar systems. To explain the difference between the two, we need to look at what is meant by "the grid." The electrical grid is the network of electrical infrastructure that connects all parts of a country, or even several countries, together. It includes generation, where energy is first produced; transmission, which is similar to the arteries transporting power to different parts of a country or country; and distribution, which takes electricity to every end-user. This electrical network is typically termed as the grid. There are standards, including quality and safety standards, that come with being tied into the grid. If you receive your power from a utility, then you are connected to the grid.

In terms of a solar system, if your solar system is connected to the grid in any way, then it is a grid-tied solution. A grid-tied solar system may or may not have a battery backup system, as you receive power from both your solar panels and the grid. This means that you don't necessarily require batteries. You need to register your solar system and have it approved by your electricity supplier. The main reason for this is that electricity suppliers need to know all the power sources on the grid. If you have a grid-tied solution, when the grid supply fails and you aren't supplied by them anymore, your system has to disconnect from the grid automatically. You can still supply power to yourself, but you cannot be connected to the grid. The reasoning behind this is simple enough. If power is turned off to a section of the grid where there is a fault, there can be nothing making that section live for safety reasons. If you haven't disconnected from the grid, you may make a grid section that needs to be worked on live. This would carry the risk of someone getting electrocuted and hurt because they are unaware of a power source. If the section is isolated, it should be safe to work on, and if it is isolated and the section is still found to be live, then figuring out where the power is coming from can waste time for those fixing the fault (August 12 & 2019, 2019).

The second option for a solar system is to have an off-grid system. In this system, the electrical network that you create is completely separate from the primary grid. You generate your own power and use it up while not connecting to the main electrical network. The advantage of this solution is that you can install your own backup battery system and be completely independent of the utility supply. In the long run, both systems will save you money. However, by using an off-grid system, the initial capital expense may be more than a grid-tied system, as you will probably need a larger solar system and would have to rewire several electrical connections. Still, in the long run, it will save you more money. This is partly because you will not be paying your monthly electricity usage, but also because you will not have to pay a maximum demand surcharge or a levy to have a connection to the utility.

The Four Main Components of a Simple Off-Grid Solar Power System

A typical off-grid solar-powered system consists of four primary components: solar panels, battery chargers, batteries, and power inverters. Each of these four components plays a vital role and works together to provide you with electricity that you can use. Other smaller components come into play, and we will get into the details of these in Chapter 2.

The solar panels are the power source of a solar system. Each panel comprises dozens of photovoltaic cells that work together and generate direct current (DC) power. They are often termed modules, panels, or solar panels. They are connected either parallel or in a series to create what is described as a solar array. A solar array generates electricity at a suitable DC voltage and current for the inverter to convert to alternating current (AC). These are two different types of electricity, and some devices can convert electricity from one type to another. The description of these two different types of electricity, AC and DC, is included in Chapter 2 below.

The second component in a solar system is the battery chargers or charge controllers. When it comes to these units, there are several options to connect to the system. There are charge controllers that use the DC electricity generated by the solar panels and charge batteries directly from this power source. There are also battery chargers that can be connected after the inverter, which charge and manage your batteries. The final option is with certain brands of inverters that have a built-in battery charger. The purpose of the battery chargers is to enable power to flow to the batteries when they are charging and from the batteries when they are discharging. Batteries are able to store energy, but must be carefully charged with energy and discharged of stored energy. The battery chargers also need to protect the batteries from being damaged by short circuits or power surges. The main reason for this is that batteries are one of the most expensive solar system components.

The third component is the batteries themselves. There are a whole host of battery types that can be used, but their function remains the same. Batteries are designed to store energy by being charged when surplus power is generated by the solar panels, such as when the sun is shining. They are then used as the source of power when insufficient energy is supplied by the solar array, such as at night. Making use of batteries creates a stable and consistent power supply from your solar system. It is proposed to oversize your solar system, especially your battery backup because you cannot predict whether you will use more power than expected or if the weather will not be conducive to generating power consistently. If you have several days of cloudy weather, then your solar panels will not be able to generate as much power compared to when it is sunny. This means that the solar panels will not meet the energy demand that you have. If you have an undersized battery backup system, then you may get by for a few days, but once the batteries have been discharged, you will be left with no power at all!

The final component of your solar system is the inverter. Inverters are devices that convert electricity from DC to AC. AC is the form of electricity that is used in all typical households. Therefore, to use the type of power that devices make use of, you need to convert the type of power that solar panels generate. Inverters use semiconductors to convert electricity and typically have a filter that gives you good quality AC supply that is safe to connect all devices to. In the US, that supply is 110 volts (V) at a frequency of 60 hertz. In many other countries worldwide, the supply power is 230 V at a frequency of 50 hertz. The type of inverter you use depends on your region and what power is used.

These four main components work in unison to give you a fully functional solar system. The solar panels, or modules, generate power from sunlight, the batteries are charged with a battery charger, the batteries themselves store energy to be used when required, and the inverter converts the electricity to the standard electrical supply used in it that region.

It is important to note that, beyond these four primary components that make up your solar system, there are also many more minor but still important things you will need to specify, design for, purchase, and install with your solar system. It is also of great importance that you thoroughly test your solar system to pick up on any defects or errors in how your system is set up and installed. Of course, it is far easier and cheaper to check for problems before you install your system at all, so making use of calculations and simulation software can greatly assist you in planning your system out. On average, you should go through three major phases in implementing your solar system, and each of these phases will take approximately the same amount of time.

Phases of Installation

The first phase is in designing your system. This includes determining where you want to install your solar system, how you want to go about the installation, and specifying the various components that you require. This includes sizing your solar panels as individual units and establishing the total number of panels that you will require. It also includes your batteries, inverter, battery charger or charge controller, tools, mounting equipment, wires, and safety practices that you should follow all the way through. You should carry out all your calculations and test your system using some form of software simulation. There are numerous software with free 30 day trials available to test if your system will work in the way you hope it will. This whole process can be called the planning phase.

The second part of your solar project is purchasing and adjudicating. You will have to research what solar panels, batteries, inverters, and charge controllers are available to you. There is no point in designing for an inverter that is readily available in Germany but extremely expensive with an extended delivery time to get to you in the US. There may also be several options that seem almost identical, and this is where you will need to adjudicate. It could be as simple as a pros and cons list to compare two different products in order to choose the best option for you. It could have a major impact on you if you go with a cheap option, only to discover laton that many of the features you require do not come with the inverter or have to be purchased separately. During this phase, you should be able to narrow down your options and purchase them from suppliers. It is imperative that you get the installation manuals with these products to ensure that you follow the manufacturer's specifications on installing the products. This phase will often lead you to a point where you realize that something you had designed for in stage one is not practically feasible, and you will have to go back to tweak your design. There is nothing wrong with this, and you shouldn't feel disheartened if you go back more than once to adjust your design to match what is available to you on the market. It's an iterative process that you want to complete in this stage, preferably before you actually purchase the equipment.

The third and final stage is the installation and testing of your solar system. If you have managed to plan out your layout, equipment, and installation method, then things should go fairly smoothly. However, in practice, there are always things that you may have missed: a tool you may require, more wires, connectors, screws, or drill bits. Nothing will ever go entirely according to plan, but the better you have planned, the fewer headaches you will have during this stage. This is often termed teething problems in engineering because a new installation will give you more trouble than a system operating for a long time. You must prepare yourself for teething problems and remain attentive to them. Sometimes, it could be something minor, such as your solar panels being dirty or a fuse blowing when you first started testing your system. Other times, the problems are a bit more challenging to overcome, such as your solar panels not being installed correctly or a large tree casting a shadow over half of your solar panels.

In this final stage, you will also need to test and monitor how your system is operating. You can use clamp meters to measure current and multimeters to measure voltage to confirm that the power you are generating is in line with what you designed for. You will also need to test any safety devices, such as isolating your solar system safely for maintenance or replacements needed later on.

These three stages form the lifecycle of your solar project and, if you follow them, spend an equal amount of time on each phase, and don't skip any major steps, then your system will be successful. You will be fully geared up to generate your own electricity, save a lot of money in the long run, and always have a backup power source should the grid go down.

Chapter 2:
Electricity 101

This chapter will go over general electricity concepts to make sense of solar systems and how to go about designing and installing them. By the end of this chapter, you should grasp the basic aspects of electricity that are relevant to solar systems.

Basic Forms of Power

To start, let us cover the two different types of electricity. These were mentioned in Chapter 1 and are known as AC and DC. AC has a voltage that alternates from positive to negative due to the charge of electrons when the power is generated, which is driven by the magnetic field. There are north and south poles of a magnet which result in the positive and negative charge. AC is named as such because the flow of electrons alternates between positive and negative. A sinusoidal wave flows along the path of electricity from the power source to where the power is used. Picture it as a wave that is generated when you throw a pebble into a pond. The waves flow away from where the pebble hits the water, and any single point experiences the water rising and falling as it moves past it. In the same way, AC electricity flows away from the power source to where the power is used. It is more straightforward to transmit AC over long distances, and it is the form of electricity that is in every household.

The other type of electricity, DC, has a continuous charge, and the voltage remains more or less stable. Instead of a wave, it is flat. DC is more stable, particularly at low voltage; therefore, many appliances and electronics use DC.

The next aspects of electricity that we will cover are that of voltage, current, and resistance:

· Voltage is measured in volts and is defined as the potential difference between two points. For example, in a car battery, the potential difference between the positive and negative terminal is 12 Volts. Voltage is the driving force behind electricity. One volt is the potential difference between two points on a wire, where one ampere of current dissipates one watt of power. This may sound confusing, but it will make sense once we cover the other aspects.

- The voltage, or potential difference, is the driving force pushing the electrons from one point to another, and the term used to describe this flow of charge is termed as the current. Thus, the current describes the rate of flow of charge from one point to another.

- The ampere, or amp for short, is the measure of current flow in electricity. In order for electricity to flow, there needs to be an exchange of electrons from one point to another. This essentially means that there is a flow of charged particles from one point to another, which is electricity.

- The next term to look into is resistance. Resistance is measured in ohms, and it resists the flow of current due to a potential difference. If it weren't for resistance in materials, we would have perfect conductors and no electricity losses. Resistance essentially takes the energy that is transmitted via electricity and wastes some of it, typically in the form of heat.

A simple way to understand the concept of these three interacting aspects of electricity is to use an analogy of something that is easier to visualize than electricity. The most common and most straightforward analogy used is that of water flowing through a pipe. In terms of water moving through a pipe, voltage is the pressure of the water, the current is the flow rate, and the diameter of the pipe is the resistance. The higher the pressure is, the faster the flow rate will be. Similarly, if there is a higher potential difference or a larger voltage, there will be an increased flow of current. The voltage would be an increase of water pressure, resulting in increased water flow given the right conditions. Do not get confused when seeing the description of potential difference and voltage used interchangeably in datasheets and other documentation, as they are the same thing when referring to electricity. However, the diameter of the pipe will limit the flow of water. A more narrow pipe represents a higher resistance. In this instance, higher pressure is required for the same flow rattan to a setup with a wider diameter pipe.

The next concept that needs to be presented is that of electrical power. Power is measured in watts and is determined by the current and voltage of a system. To calculate the power, you only need to multiply the current and the voltage. The power determines how much energy is being transferred from the source to the load at any given time. For example, if a 12 V battery is driving a 2 A current across a load, then the power delivered to the load is the two multiplied by each other, or 24 W.

The Difference Between Power and Energy

The power measured in watts describes how much energy is used up at any given time, so when you see a light bulb that is 100 W, you know that it uses more energy every second than a 60 W light bulb. Total energy use is calculated by multiplying the power supplied in one moment by the amount of time power was supplied. However, this is different from how most energy meters work. When you receive an electrical bill, the amount of energy you use is not given to you in the units of energy, which is joules. It seems unusual that you aren't charged for the exact amount of energy you used, so why is that?

The short answer is that it is too complicated to measure the power flow at every single instance and determine its energy. Instead, what is used is referred to as watt-hours (Wh).

When you are charged from your utility, the bill will typically describe the energy used up as kilowatt hours (kWh). A kilo represents a unit of 1,000, so 1,000 Wh is the same as 1 kWh. We are all charged in kWh from the utility because this is an average amount of energy that we use and not the precise amount itself. Typically, energy meters sample the amount of power being used once every 15 minutes. This means that four samples are taken over the span of an hour, and they all contribute to the overall amount of energy estimated (Enphase, n.d.).

An analogy to describe the difference between watts and watt-hours, which is essentially the difference between power and energy, is looking at speed and distance. Power is the rate of flow of energy, just as speed is the rate of change of distance. So, if you are driving at 60 mph, that would be equivalent to the power. If you were to drive for 30 minutes at this speed in a single direction, then you should cover 30miles, and this would be the equivalent of the energy. The faster you go, the more distance you can cover. Similar to the higher power you have, the more energy you can transfer.

When it comes to batteries, the measurement of energy available is typically provided in ampere-hours (Ah). This, again, can be translated into energy, as energy is the product of power and time. If, for example, you have a car battery, which is typically 12 V, and are given a rating of 200 Ah as the battery rating, then you can determine the energy stored by multiplying amp hours by the voltage, so 200 x 12, which is 6,000 Wh of 6 kWh of energy. The reason for this type of measurement is that it makes it easier to determine how long your batteries last. If you have the same 200 Ah battery and have several devices that you wish to power from it, you only need to look at how much current these devices draw to know how long the battery will last. For example, if you have lights and some devices connected to plugs and you work out that you will need 20 A of current, you only need to determine how much power you can draw from the battery. Theoretically, a battery being rated at 200 Ah should be able to supply 20 A for 10 hours. This will be covered in more detail in Chapter 2 when we discuss deep cycles for batteries.

Another important feature of electrical systems is protection. Protection is self-explanatory, and multiple protection devices are used to protect both people and electrical devices. Examples of protection devices are circuit breakers and fuses. When there is an electrical fault or a short circuit, these protection devices will be activated—circuit breakers trip to isolate the power to prevent any further damage or harm done to people. Think of them as a light switch that turns the power off automatically when it detects too much current flow to the load. When it comes to fuses, they will burn out instantly to open the circuit and stop the current from flowing when there is too much current flowing through them. Both fuses and circuit breakers typically have a rating that tells you how much current they will allow to flow through them and when they will operate to protect the electrical devices.

Basics on Solar Systems

Now that we have covered some of the basic elektricity terms, let's take a closer look at solar systems in particular and all the required components. You can connect panels to form what is called a string. A string of panels is typically made up of several panels connected in series. In electricity, the two main ways of connecting a circuit are called series-connected and parallel-connected components. A series connection links one component to another to form a big loop, whereas a parallel connection links components together like the steps of a ladder. All components are connected to the same line on each side.

When you connect a string of solar panels, if you opt for a DC charge controller, it is important to have fuses at the point of connection to the inverter and charge controller of the batteries. These fuses will protect the inverter, battery charger, and other solar panels if there is a short circuit.

Strings of solar panels work together to increase the voltage and boost the amount of generated power. The more solar panels that you have, the more power you can generate. Most inverters are equipped with multiple inputs from the solar panels to allow several strings of panels to be connected.

There is also certain terminology that you will need to be familiar with regarding electrical infrastructure relating to your solar system. The first of these things is a distribution board (DB). This is basically where your power is distributed to the different loads. All houses have a DB with an incomer from the utility, metering of some kind for the utility to track and charge you for your electricity usage, and feeders that feed power to your home's different areas. The concept is the same for an off-grid solar system. All your AC power will have to be fed from this single location. DBs typically have an incomer from your power source, which will be your inverter in this case. The incomer is typically a circuit breaker that is often called your main breaker. You will then find smaller circuit breakers that feed the different areas that require power. Lights are usually fed from what is known as a single-pole circuit breaker, and plugs, geysers, stoves, and other major loads are fed from double pole circuit breakers. A double pole circuit breaker has both a live and neutral connection from the circuit breaker to the loads, whereas single pole circuit breakers only have the live connection.

There is also typically an earth leakage unit that is designed to protect from earth faults in your system, an earth bar, a neutral bar, and a protected neutral bar. An earth leakage device is a device that is designed to protect you from getting electrocuted. It detects the current flowing to a load and returning from it, as electricity has to circulate in a loop. If it is detected that the current flowing to your loads does not match the current flowing back from them, it is assumed that there is a discharge to earth through a person or device. This is hazardous and could potentially injure a person, so when this situation is detected, the power is isolated completely. A DB is sometimes called a fuse box or feeder panel depending on the size and functionality, but they refer to the same fundamental thing.

An inverter is a device that converts the DC power that is generated from your solar system or batteries into AC power for you to use for plug points, appliances, and lighting. They are one of the core components of your solar system, alongside the batteries, battery charger, and solar panels. Inverters make use of semiconductive devices, and they have a limit to their efficiency. Be careful when sizing your solar system, as the power generated by your solar panels will not be 100% available for you to use in your AC system. A good rule of thumb to use is to take an efficiency of 85%, meaning that, of the power generated by your solar panels, only 85% will be available to use. This will help you avoid any issues in the future when you realize that you aren't able to get as much power out of your solar system as you originally expected.

When it comes to solar systems, there is a term known as peak sun hours (PSH), which effectively allows you to calculate how much power you can get from your solar panels on an average day. Although there may be 12 hours of sunlight on an average day, you may only have a listing of seven hours of PSH, as your panels will not be generating 100% power over the full 12 hours. Instead, there may be five hours of fully efficient production of electricity and four hours of partial efficiency, resulting in only seven hours of full productivity. In the four hours of partial sun exposure, you may get approximately 50% of the sun intensity and photons you would receive during the middle of the day. This means that the four hours of 50% sun intensity translate to two hours of PSH.

When you determine the amount of power that you can get from your panels, you shouldn't use the number of hours of sunlight during the day, but, rather, the number of PSH. This is also important for seasonal changes as your panels will inevitably have fewer PSH during the winter months when compared to the summer months.

Another concept that isn't often discussed is the power factor. Power is technically measured as apparent power, also known as active power, which makes up the watts that we are now familiar with, and the second type of power is known as reactive power. Reactive power is a power that doesn't show active use and is a part of your power that you want to reduce as far as possible. All inductive loads, such as stoves and geysers, have a component of inductance that demands reactive power. This power isn't obviously shown in your active power or watt usage, making it confusing sometimes when you look at your power demand and solar system capability and see a gap between the two. It's not easy to explain, but the basics are that a voltage is set up, and the current follows it. The greater the lag between the voltage set up and the flow of current is determined by induction, and the further behind the current lags, the lower your power factor and the more power is lost without delivering useful energy. The most typical way that reactive power is compensated for is by using filter devices such as capacitors. They are commonly used in larger-scale electrical systems but are costly and are not used often in residential applications.

Solar inverters are designed to supply your load based on its requirements. If you have large inductive loads, the chances are that you will have what is known as a poor power factor. Power factor is basically a ratio between the different forms of power. A typical load will have a power factor ranging from 0 to 1.0. A value of 1.0 is outstanding. It means that your ratio of apparent power, measured in volt-amps (VA), is exactly equal to your active, or real, power with a ratio of one to one. It may seem confusing since the ratio is not linear and is a root mean squared ratio. That being said, a power factor of 0.8 is terrible, whereas a power factor of 0.95 is very good. This translates to 80% of your power being used in a useful way versus 95% of your power being used in a useful way.

This is an important aspect to cover because your inverters will put out power to cater to loads of a certain size, but that doesn't consider the type of load you are connecting. If you are unaware of this theory, then you may end up underestimating the size of your inverter, expecting it to power loads that it simply isn't adequate for. No system will have a perfect power factor; thus, a lot of the power that your inverter will generate goes into this "wasted" energy that hasn't been accounted for. When configuring your inverter, you will typically be able to see the amount of real and reactive power that you are generating but not be able to compensate for this. There are devices known as power factor correction banks, but these are designed more for larger-scale systems.

In terms of power factor for your solar system, just assume that it accounts for a reduction in efficiency between the power that your inverter can generate and the power demand of your load. In this way, it will not take you by surprise later on when you aren't getting out what you expected.

There is also an aspect known as insulation. The insulation of a material is the opposite of the conductivity. If something is a good insulator, then it is a very poor conductor and vice versa. This is specific to electricity in this case, as conductivity could be for several other things, such as heat. It is important to have good insulation materials for things that should not be live. This includes the insulation material that surrounds cables and all components that shield you from live conductors. How well a material can withstand and protect you from live conductors is known as the insulation voltage rating. This is different for AC and DC voltages, as explained below.

The process of converting DC power into AC power is known as inverting the power. The process of converting AC power into DC power is termed rectifying the power. When the process takes place, the voltage that you get on one side does not match the other side, i.e., 1 V of AC power does not become 1 V of DC power once it has been rectified. This is true for both the rectifying and inverting process. The DC voltage equivalent from rectifying AC can be calculated with the following simple equation:

Voltage Insulation Rating (DC) = Voltage Insulation Rating (AC) / 2

This implies that an insulation material that can protect you from 1,000V of AC power can only protect you from 700 V of DC power. It's important to know this difference so that you don't specify an insulator or any equipment with an insulation rating in AC and expect it to work for the same DC voltage.

Another aspect to consider with designing, purchasing, installing, and testing your solar system is to look at engineering firms that carry out these projects daily. There are many lessons that you can take from them when building your own system. It's easier to learn from other's mistakes or best practices than to have to go through the trouble yourself. One practice that is often skipped in do-it-yourself projects is having a design review of some kind. If you have designed your own system, you may not be aware of any gaps in your design or things that you may not have considered that are commonplace in solar systems. Engineering companies will hold internal reviews where a team of experts gives feedback on one person's design. The design will be scrutinized to determine whether the solution makes sense technically, legally, ethically, that it meets quality standards, and that it is, indeed, the best fit solution for the requirements at hand. A good idea is to discuss your design with someone who has carried out their own solar system before and get input. It can be expanded into getting multiple opinions on your design and plans. It isn't about changing your design completely because someone else has a different opinion on how you should do things. It is more of a guideline to help you think laterally and think of things that may have slipped through the cracks when you carried out the design of your system. Again, it is far easier and cheaper to make changes to your design before it has materialized than after!

Chapter 3:
How To Choose The Right Battery

When it comes to figuring out which battery to use for your solar system, you need to know what different batteries are available on the market and the pros and cons of the different types of batteries. You may think you are getting a great deal on cheap batteries only to find that they don't perform well and only last you two to three years before failing. You may look at the price tag of a high-end battery and feel as though you are being ripped off only to find that it is a deep cycle battery that performs well and lasts you over ten years. It's all about selecting the best option for the right price.

It's important to remember, once again, that the cost of something isn't purely about the price tag that you see when you first purchase something. The cost of ownership should also be compared. If you have a maintenance-free battery, then you will save on maintenance costs. Also, if you have an expensive battery option that lasts you ten years and another is half the cost but only lasts for three years, you will save in the long run by going for the more expensive battery.

Let's begin by explaining what a deep cycle battery is. Batteries are basically devices that store energy. They require charging in order to absorb the energy. When this power is needed, the batteries discharge to supply the power. The process of charging and discharging is not perfect, and there are losses experienced. Due to the physical construction of batteries, they cannot be discharged to 0% charge. Standard batteries can only discharge to 60% charge, meaning that only 40% of the energy stored in the batteries can be accessed. Deep cycle batteries can discharge 80% of their stored energy, which is significantly more than standard batteries. However, in order to ensure that the lifespan of the batteries is per manufacturer specifications, you shouldn't discharge them beyond a 45% charge. If you stick to this, you will be able to use the batteries for a much longer time. When you discharge the battery to its limit, there is internal degradation of the batteries, which means that they will never be able to store as much energy as before. The more you cycle beyond the point specified, the more degradation will occur until the batteries will not be able to charge at all. This will inevitably happen with all batteries, but it is better to have batteries last for five years than overwork them and last only three years (Crown Battery, 2018).

When it comes to deep cycle batteries, you can cycle the charge and discharge amounts at a much higher rate than other battery types. Most batteries will also have a rated number of cycles guaranteed, which is an important factor to take into consideration when selecting a battery. Some will guarantee up to 500 cycles, which would result in less than two years of daily use. Others will guarantee as many as 2,500 cycles, meaning they will last you much longer even if you are discharging them more than once per day (Energy Matters, n.d.).

Two additional categories describe the different types of deep cycle batteries. These are sealed type, or maintenance-free batteries, and flooded deep cycle batteries. Flooded deep cycle batteries require inspection and maintenance. For lead-acid batteries, which are the most commonly used, there is a minimum and maximum level of electrolytic liquid. When the liquid drops below the minimum level, they need to be topped up with distilled water. Many batteries are described as sealed type batteries, but aren't truly sealed batteries. This is specifically true for absorbed glass mat (AGM) batteries, which are actually valve regulated and not truly sealed. In fact, most sealed type batteries are actually valve regulated. As another example, lead acid batteries give off hydrogen gas over time, specifically when they charge, and this gas builds up pressure in the batteries. This is why, instead of being completely sealed, these batteries have a valve to allow the gas to be released before the internal pressure gets to a dangerous level.

There are also different types of batteries that work using different principles. The most common types of batteries used for energy storage are lithium-ion, flooded lead-acid, AGM, and gel batteries. Each of these primary types of batteries have pros and cons, which are essential to know for you to decide what will best fit your requirements.

Lithium-Ion Batteries

Lithium-ion batteries are one of the most commonly used batteries used today. They are lightweight compared to other batteries, which explains why they are used in many electronic devices such as cell phones, tablets, and laptops. They are incredibly durable and are more resilient to harsh weather conditions than other batteries. They also last the longest of the five battery types mentioned above, and they require very little or no maintenance at all. The batteries themselves are sealed, so it is mostly the connections that need to be checked once in a while to see if the battery is still charging and discharging adequately. The batteries are also compact and don't take up a lot of space, which is great when this is a factor to consider, such as in an RV or on a boat.

The disadvantage when it comes to lithium-ion batteries is that they are costly. A typical, deep-cycle lithium-ion battery will cost about four times as much as the other options that will be discussed. That being said, they will last the longest out of all of the batteries, with many being rated to last between 10 and 15 years. Another drawback with lithium-ion batteries is that they are sensitive to electrical faults and need to be protected against them, particularly voltage surges. They are also sensitive to temperature and will not last as long in high temperatures (above 25 degrees Celsius, or 77 degrees Fahrenheit). This means that they need to be stored in a cool, dry area to maximize their lifespan. Another issue comes with disposing of lithium-ion batteries. If a lithium-ion battery is pierced, it can be explosive. This is why manufacturers of lithium-ion batteries take every precaution possible to ensure any failure is sealed by having protective plates. However, if these batteries were to end up in a dump, the risk increases. This means that, after the batteries stop working, there is a small expense for specialists to dispose of them responsibly.

Flooded Lead Acid Batteries

The next battery that we will look at is the flooded lead acid battery. As previously mentioned, they do require regular inspection and maintenance. They have been around for a long time and are known to be reliable hence car batteries today still make use of lead acid batteries. They are also used in battery tripping units in almost every substation in the world for backup power to protect devices connecting the grid.

One of the most significant advantages of these types of batteries is that they can supply a large amount of power quickly without damage to the batteries. If you turn on a device with an element such as a kettle, geyser, or toaster, the power drawn spikes as a large amount of current is needed to power these devices. These batteries are able to supply this demand without it affecting the quality of the power being delivered. They are also cheap in comparison to the other types of batteries on this list. If you have several different large loads that you will be turning on and off regularly, these batteries may be the option you are looking for. Although these batteries require maintenance, they have a relatively simple design and are easy to repair.

The disadvantage with these batteries is that they contain a liquid with a cap keeping the liquid in, but they need to be kept upright, and it is not advisable to move them often. Although they typically have a cap to keep the liquid from spilling over, it is not a vacuum seal, and the electrolytic liquid will leak if the batteries are moved often. Also, as mentioned, they require frequent inspection and topping up with distilled water when the electrolytic liquid drops below the minimum threshold. They also have a low energy density, meaning that they don't store a large amount of energy for their physical size and weight. This type of battery also gives off hydrogen gas as they charge, which is flammable. This isn't a problem when they are stored in an area with good ventilation, but if they are stored in a sealed room, the buildup of hydrogen can be dangerous.

These batteries also have the risk of chemical burns as they do contain acid. It is crucial that these batteries are stored upright so as not to leak this acidic electrolytic liquid. The term "electrolytic", for the liquid contained in batteries, is used because these batteries use a process known as electrolysis to store a charge. When the batteries are charging, electrolysis occurs, which converts the chemicals into ions and anions, which are the batteries' positive and negatively charged elements. These then combine to form a single compound, and this process is used to store and release energy. Chemical processes require energy. In certain chemical processes, energy is released when different elements combine. This change of energy levels is what is analyzed when determining what compounds could potentially make for good batteries. Other conditions are considered as well when selecting what chemicals to make use of in batteries. Such as the chemical process taking place at room temperature, how easy it is to reverse the process, and whether or not degradation can be minimized so the chemical process can be reversed and repeated many times. Batteries are chemical reactions in a mostly closed system and store and release energy in the form of electricity when we require it.

There is also the risk of thermal runaway where the batteries are overused and overheat, which results in dangerously high temperatures for the electrolytic material. This is an extremely infrequent occurrence, and battery manufacturers design their batteries to reduce this risk as far as practically possible. If your batteries are not operating correctly and are running hot, then it is highly recommended that you remove them from the operation. This rare occurrence will occur when there is a defect in a battery; therefore, if this were to happen to one of your batteries, it would likely only be in one of the batteries in your battery bank. A warranty claim can almost always be made in this instance, provided you are storing your batteries correctly and in accordance with the manufacturer's specifications.

Valve Regulated or Sealed Batteries

The final battery is the valve regulated, or sealed, battery. These come in two main forms: AGM and gel type batteries. Unlike the flooded lead acid batteries, these units are self-contained and require no real maintenance, only an inspection from time to time. The most significant advantage of these batteries is that they can hold their charge for a very long time, unlike most batteries which discharge over time. Think of a car that has been standing for a few weeks, but it still has enough charge to start the car. That ability to hold charge while not being used over extended periods of time is a massive benefit with these batteries. This makes them ideal for solar systems that aren't used daily, such as in RVs. They are self-contained and give off only trace amounts of hydrogen over time. They are also significantly cheaper than lithium-ion batteries, which are also sealed batteries that do not spill. The final advantage of these batteries is that they are non-hazardous, making them safer to dispose of than lithium-ion batteries.

One of the disadvantages associated with these batteries is that they are more expensive than flooded lead acid batteries. They also don't last as long as lithium-ion batteries, resulting in their demand decreasing over time. They are bulkier than lithium-ion batteries and have a shorter lifespan.

AGM batteries, in particular, are incredibly robust and can handle movement and shock. This is why they are used as car batteries in almost all internal combustion engine vehicles. These batteries can also charge to a full charge at a lower voltage than specified. This means that even a 12 V rated battery can be fully charged with a 10 V supply voltage, which is hugely advantageous. They can also handle the high current without being damaged. AGM batteries can be charged quicker than other batteries and can give a deep cycle discharge when power is needed. This makes them just as popular as lithium-ion batteries for solar solutions, especially when it comes to mobile applications such as RV's, boats, and trailers for camping.

Gel batteries, like AGM batteries, are robust and resistant to shock and are also maintenance-free apart from inspections. They also have the advantage of not leaking even if their physical construction is compromised. They are incredibly resilient in extreme temperatures, making them functional even in extreme weather conditions, such as low or high temperatures, high humidity, or high altitude. These batteries can be transported without issues and operate normally, even when on their side or upside down. Because of their extreme resilience to extreme weather, they are often used in marine and aircraft applications.

However, gel batteries are not as popular when it comes to solar solutions because they are far more expensive than AGM batteries with similar properties. They are also extremely sensitive to how they are charged and can be damaged easily electrically, despite being robust physically. They also don't cycle as deeply as other batteries and are large and heavy for the amount of energy they can store.

The Takeaway

The two most advantageous battery options to consider for your solar solution are lithium-ion batteries and AGM batteries. They are the two most prominent players in the market because they are better suited for off-grid solar systems than the other battery types.

Of course, the capital expenditure on these batteries is constantly changing, but, at present, AGM batteries cost between US$300 and US$500 for a 12V, 200Ah unit. In comparison, lithium-ion batteries with similar ratings will cost between US$1,200 and US$1,500. This clearly shows the advantage of AGM batteries from a cost-saving perspective, but the trade-off comes with the depth of discharge and number of cycles that the batteries are capable of. AGM batteries for this price will typically be able to discharge and charge around 400 times, while lithium-ion batteries can discharge approximately 2,000 times. Although the AGM batteries are a third of the price, the lithium-ion batteries will last five times as long.

Chapter 4:
How To Choose The Right Solar Panel

Choosing the right solar panel for you may seem a bit daunting, especially in an age where there are more options than we know what to do with. In order to figure out what will work best for you, you need to ask a few questions so you can decide for yourself. There is so much information available online and in the market, so it is helpful to know what to look out for and what to avoid when making your decision. Everyone has an opinion on what's best for you, and worse than that is someone in sales trying to sell a specific product to you. Unfortunately, all salespeople will want to sell a product that they have, so you need to take what they say with a grain of salt. You should be informed of the positives and negatives of any solar panel option, as the salesperson for a specific panel will not give you the negatives that their solar panel has.

Solar panels are all rated according to standard test conditions (STC). This means that all ratings you will find listed on solar panel datasheets for performing and are expected to perform are provided at STC levels. This includes a temperature of 25 degrees Celsius, or 77 degrees Fahrenheit; an altitude at sea level, or less than 1,000m or 3,280 ft; low levels of humidity; and an average amount of solar radiation reaching the earth. Solar radiation intensity determines just how much energy is available at any given location to convert into electricity via the photovoltaic process.

The average used is 1,000 W per square meter. This means that for every square meter of space, or just under 11 square feet, there is 1,000 W of potential power available to convert to electricity using standard PV solar panels, regardless of what type. This is the rating according to direct solar radiation, which is added to via indirect solar radiation. This includes all reflected light off of other surfaces, including pavements and buildings, which increases solar radiation levels by a small amount. This level differs from one location to another depending on the amount of sunlight received in that place.

The amount of solar radiation that is available to you is determined by your geographical location. There are online resources available that indicate the intensity of solar radiation for every place on earth. NASA is to thank for a lot of this data that is available to us. Many locations are fortunate to have a much higher solar radiation available per unit area, and can generate a lot more power with the same number of panels than locations with average solar radiation levels. However, many of these areas also experience high average daily temperatures, which results in the de-rating of the solar panel's ability to generate power. In many instances, these two factors balance out and the benefits of a higher solar radiation intensity don't impact the solar power generation levels of these solar arrays. This means that a desert-mounted solar panel cannot necessarily generate more power than a rooftop installation in France. It's all about associating your solar radiation levels with temperature and where you are in making use of this solar system. If you experience very little direct sunlight, you are likely to draw a much lower level of energy from your solar panels than people living in high solar radiation areas.

Solar panels will generate the most amount of electricity when they are directly facing the sun. This essentially maximizes the surface area of the panels that can be exposed to photons. This means that when you install your solar panels, it is beneficial to have them exposed to the most amount of sunlight throughout the day. Apart from shadows and other potential obstructions that could reduce the amount of sunlight received by the panels, the angle at which you mount them is crucial. This is determined by what is known as the azimuth. The azimuth describes the angle at which the sun rises and sets on the east to west path. Your latitude will change the sun's angle in the sky, and you will want to tilt your panels to face the sun at the highest rate possible. This means that, in the northern hemispheres, such as in the US, your angles will be tilted to face more towards the south rather than lying flat. The opposite is experienced for locations in the southern hemisphere. The general rule of thumb is to take your coordinates, more specifically your latitude, and add 15 degrees for summer and subtract 15 degrees for winter. This is for situations where you intend to adjust the tilt angle of your solar panels from season to season. This action will not affect your energy generation capacity by more than 5%; therefore, many people opt to mount their solar systems at the same latitude angle on a rigid mounting structure and do not adjust between seasons (De Rooij, 2020).

The key is to narrow down your selection so that you know what makes sense and what doesn't. If you want to install a permanent installation on the roof of your home, then your requirements will vary from if you want to put up a few panels on an RV to power you as you take a road trip.

The first thing that you need to ask yourself is what your application will be. Will you have a fixed solar installation in the same set location, such as on the roof of your home, or a mobile solar system on a car, boat, RV, or camping trailer. Think of this as a mobile or non-mobile solution moving forward. The mobile solution needs to be durable and robust enough to handle vibration and other mechanical shocks without being damaged. Non-mobile solutions do not need to be as resilient to vibration, but will need to be strong enough to handle various weather conditions, such as hail storms, without being damaged.

There are two predominant divisions of solar panels available on the market today. They are monocrystalline and polycrystalline. The difference between these two options is in their manufacturing. Monocrystalline solar cells are manufactured from a single silicon crystals, whereas polycrystalline panels are manufactured from several silicon crystals combined. This means that monocrystalline panels are much more expensive because they require a lot more manufacturing finesse in order to keep them uniform. This leads to them being more energy-efficient but a lot more expensive. Over 90% of the solar panels installed today are polycrystalline because they are around 80% as efficient in capturing energy, but they are far cheaper. A typical monocrystalline solar panel will have an energy capturing capacity of around 25%, making them the most efficient solar panel per unit area. They are mostly used in installations where space is limited, but the price isn't a concern. In comparison, a polycrystalline solar panel will have a typical efficiency of 20%, making them substantially less efficient but far cheaper. This level of efficiency may sound extremely low, but that is the amount of energy captured from the sun per unit area, and that number is growing as the materials and technology we apply improve over time.

There are also flexible and rigid solar panel options. Rigid solar panels are designed to be installed as they are on rooftops or mounted in such a way that their bulky structure is not intrusive. Flexible solar panels are designed to be lightweight and compact so that they can streamline a design. This is why flexible solar panels are used in cars and boats more often than in other applications. Once again, they make up a very small market segment because they are considerably more costly. They are also more susceptible to damage from impact, whereas rigid solar panels are designed to be more robust.

Let's take a look at a rooftop installation on an RV as an example to weigh the pros and cons of using a rigid or flexible solar solution. The immediate and obvious advantage of using flexible solar panels over rigid ones in this installation is that they are much lighter and won't weigh the vehicle down. Another massive advantage is that they don't require a bulky frame to mount the panels on and have much less impact on the vehicle's fuel efficiency, as they don't all have a lot of drag. In comparison, rigid solar panels mounted on the roof require a mounting structure and are large panels themselves. These factors combined mean that there will be a lot more drag on the vehicle when driven, and the additional weight will further degrade fuel efficiency. Rigid panels are typically four to five times heavier than flexible panels.

The advantage of rigid solar panels is that they can be moved or adjusted in order to be directed towards the sun, maximizing the power generated. Flexible panels are typically mounted flush to the surface of a vehicle, which means that you cannot adjust the angle of the panels to face the sun directly. Fortunately, there is a technology that is present for flexible solar panels. This is basically raised dots on the panel to improve the solar capturing capability of the panels. However, this is still less effective than simply aiming the panel to face the sun directly, which is more practical than the rigid panels.

The rigid solar panels are very durable, so they are more resistant to scratches to the panels from things like branches. This means that flexible panels are more likely to get damaged in this way than rigid solar panels. The option you pick is purely based on your requirement and budget, as both of these panel types are tried and tested in multiple industries.

In terms of permanently installed panels that will not be moved, such as on houses or panels that are moved to a location and positioned, such as camping trailers, the energy generated per unit area is critical. Many solar panels are 2m long and 1m wide, or roughly 6.5 ft long and 3.5 ft wide, with varying energy generation capabilities. Some of these units will be rated at 250 W, and others at 400 W. It is beneficial to use panels that have a higher energy density, which means that they can generate more power per unit area. These panels are made up of higher efficiency cells, or energy cells that are packed more tightly on a solar panel and hence can generate more power per unit area (Matasci, 2019).

Every solar panel is made up of a string of solar cells that are connected together. Because these cells are typically connected together in series, they all need to be operational for the solar panel to generate power. If there is an open circuit between cells, then the panel will not generate electricity. Many panels have built-in components to try and minimize this risk and still generate some power even if there is damage to one of the cells. For this same reason, solar panels will lose power generated when there is shading. It only takes one cell out of dozens, of which there are typically 72 but can be as high as 96, being in a shadow to reduce the power generated by the entire solar panel. This is because less current is permitted to flow in the entire panel, which can drop the power output by as much as 60%. It is a huge issue to have shading on your solar panel if even a tiny portion of the panel can result in such a huge loss in power generation. Again, there are technologies available to reduce the impact of partial shading on solar panels, but this comes with additional cost. Many solar panels have built-in diodes and other devices which manage power loss far better than standard solar panels. If you run the risk of your solar panels being partly shaded regularly, such as from trees around the solar system, it is worth looking into these types of solar panels.

Always be sure to look out for brands that are internationally accredited. There is no use in bargaining on a solar panel that seems to be of a price that is too good to be true. Suppose the main brands that you recognize, such as CanadaSolar, Jinko, or Trina, are far more expensive than another brand. In that case, it is likely a scam or a product that hasn't met international standards. As with all things in technology, inferior products will not last long, and you will end up wasting your money and have to upgrade later to the units with a standard price.

The most common symbols to look out for on a product to ensure it meets international safety or quality standards are the CE or UL marks. The CE mark stands for "Conformitè Europëenne," European body that confirms that a product meets the body's requirements in terms of safety and quality. Products manufactured or distributed in Europe have to have this marking to represent the quality. In the USA, however, these markings are not compulsory for products being distributed. Many manufacturers still opt to put these symbols on their products to sell their products as good quality products. The UL symbol stands for "Underwriters Laboratories," which indicates that Underwriters Laboratories has inspected samples of the product. They have determined that it conforms to their safety standards. When you are looking for panels to purchase for your solar system, always look for these symbols. Stick to the products that show these labels to know that you are getting a product that has been scrutinized and was found to be safe.

When selecting a solar panel type, you will need to look at what is readily available from solar panel suppliers where you plan to purchase the panels. There are often shortages of a specific size due to large projects buying up all of the availability of certain panels. There are multiple brands that you can choose from, and you will often find that a large order has been placed which hasn't been fully collected, or an excess of panels was ordered for a large client. This could lead to excellent deals and discounted costs on certain panel types. At this stage, it's important for you to look at whether the availability and cost of panels on the market matches the design that you have put together for your solar system. If you specified polycrystalline, 360 W panels, but there is an excellent price for polycrystalline, 320 W panels, then it may be worthwhile to go for the cheaper option, even if you do lose out on some of the power output from each panel. Go back to your original design and see whether this change in panel selection will have an impact, especially if you have to purchase more panels than you had initially intended.

Electrical systems also tend to have a rating that decreases when you go above an altitude of 1,000 m, or 3,280 ft, above sea level. This may impact your installation if you plan to install or make use of it above this level. The same goes for temperature and humidity. Solar panels have a derating above 25 degrees Celsius or 77 degrees Fahrenheit. The depreciation is linear up until approximately 75 degrees Celsius or 167 degrees Fahrenheit. Suppose you experience high temperatures during the summer months. In that case, you may experience a derating factor and only end up generating 90% of the possible power output of the solar panels themselves. It is crucial to consult the specific solar panel datasheet that you plan on using in order to see these values and be realistic in specifying your system.

Solar panels also deteriorate over time due to the photovoltaic effect. Typical panels are tagged with a lifespan of 25 years, and, at that point, they will only be able to generate 40% of the power they were originally rated for. This deterioration is also approximately linear over time, so even after ten years of operation, your panels will only generate around 80% of the power they were in year one. A solar system is a long-term investment, so having this information is important when looking far into the future at the benefits that come from making use of them. It's not to say that after 25 years the solar panels will not continue working for many years after that. It is more relevant to power generation plants that use tens of thousands of solar panels. This loss of possible revenue makes the solar plant non-profitable after 25 years if the panels aren't completely replaced. You could still have a solar system on your house working after 40 years.

This rating is also a conservative average that manufacturers specify and does not equate to every single panel deteriorating at the same rate. There are many pros to using solar panels, but it requires that you fully understand the current limitations of the products in the market today.

When connecting solar panels to form a string, you will need connecting wires and clips, most commonly the MC4 clips, which have a male and female connection and clip tightly when pushed together. Most solar panels are manufactured to have short lengths of wires, with one wire connected with a male clip and another with a female clip. This makes it easier to discern between the positive and negative terminals. It is essential to connect the positive of one panel into the negative of the adjacent unit and form a string. If you connect a panel the wrong way around, then the voltages will cancel out, and it could damage the internal cells of the solar panel. Fortunately, most units have built-in diodes, which are electronic components that only allow current to flow in one direction and not the other. These diodes prevent current from flowing through one panel, keeping it from running through the entire string of panels.

When you are specifying a solar panel for your application, confirm that the solar panel has these wire leads with the MC4 clips on them. Also, make sure that the leads are long enough to reach between two panels that are mounted right next to each other. Older solar panel models were often supplied with a terminal box with a positive and negative connection point without these cable lengths, meaning that more materials would need to be purchased, and installing the units becomes more labor-intensive. There is no point in saving cost on your solar panels by selecting units without wire leads, known as tails, and ending up spending more when combining the cost of the wires, clips, and solar panels than a more expensive solar panel that comes with these components included.

The same goes for mounting clips. Something as small as having pre-drilled holes for mounting brackets to be used to secure your solar panels can save you time and expendable parts, such as drill bits. Modern solar panels come with an aluminum frame built around the cells. These frames typically have a lip, which means that they can be clamped to a structure and no drilling will be required for the solar panel itself. This maintains its integrity and reduces the risk of accidentally drilling through the protective glass and creating a weak spot in it. Be sure to look for solar panels with this frame if you have selected to use rigid solar panels.

Chapter 5:
How To Choose The Right Wires, Fuses, and Inverter

Now that we have sized the solar system that you require, determined which batteries will suit your application, and established which solar panels will be the best fit, it's time to look at all the other major components you will require for your solar system. This chapter will focus on sizing and selecting your inverter, fuses for protection, and cables to connect the panels, inverter, battery, and loads. It will then expand this to typical mounting structures that are used for various applications. In Chapter 6, the process of installing and testing your solar system will be covered, so the mounting structures presented in this chapter are just to help you select the right units for your requirements.

Sizing Your Cables and Wires

To start, the cables that you use have a significant impact on your solar system. There are specific single-core cables that are required to use for DC systems. Cables rated to handle 1,000 V of AC power aren't necessarily suited to use in DC circuits. When looking at cable options, make sure that you select one with a DC-rated voltage and ensure that the string of solar panels you have to connect to your inverter does not exceed this DC voltage. The current rating of the cable that you require is also extremely important. If you have a string of panels that will supply 10 A, then the cable you select needs to be rated at 10 A or higher. It is advisable to select a cable that is one size larger than the rated current that you require. This is to ensure that they can handle a short circuit current. Fortunately, with solar systems, the fault current is very close to the full load current of the solar panels. This is because they cannot supply excess power to a short circuit, unlike many other sources, such as generators.

Another consideration that you need to look at is the length of the cables from the solar panels to your inverter. The longer a cable is, the more internal resistance they have and the more power losses you will experience. There is a phenomenon known as voltage drop on cables due to length. Most solar systems are designed to have the inverter close to the panels, so your cable length shouldn't be long enough to create a voltage drop across them. When selecting an AC cable to be installed on the output of your inverter to a distribution board, this may be a consideration that you have to look at. We will cover this once we complete the requirements to consider in your DC cables.

When considering the type of cable you require, it's essential to think about the nature of the installation. Some cables are manufactured with protective armoring, which is useful for cables buried in the ground or mounted where they could experience an impact that risks cutting into the cable. The downside of an armored cable is that it is more expensive and more rigid. It's far easier to bend an unarmoured cable, making it easier to install. A word of caution here: All cables have a minimum bending radius. This means that if you need to bend a 90 degree angle in the cable, you have to bend it in a curve rather than put a 90 degree bend on the cable, as this will damage it and create a weak spot. All cables have this bending radius listed on a datasheet for reference. It's usually given in inches or millimeters and assists you ininstalling the cables according to the manufacturer's specifications.

Another consideration is in using cables that are resistant to ultraviolet (UV) light. The sun gives off UV light, and this can degrade cables over time. Cables that are not resistant to UV light will become hard and crack. If a crack goes from the outer cable to the live conductor inside, then you may experience a fault or risk being electrocuted if you touch this part of the cable. As all solar panels need to be mounted outdoors in order to capture the sunlight, selecting UV-resistant cables is recommended.

Most solar panels are manufactured with lengths of positive and negative cables with connector clips on them. These cable lengths are known as tails, and the cables that you select should connect to these tails. A lot of the time, solar panels have tails that are long enough to connect panels to either side of it to form the strings, and you only need to connect to the first and last panel in a string to connect it to the inverter. This saves cost on cables and connector clips.

You will need to make sure that the cable you select will be able to fit the right connector clip on it to connect to the solar panel clips. These clips have a range of wire sizes that will fit them and are designed to fit into all the common cable sizes typically used in solar installations.

A typical cable that you could select would be a 2.5mm2, single-core, unarmoured, 1,000 voltage in direct current (VDC), UV resistant cable. Many datasheets are available from different cable manufacturers, including Aberdare and Lapp, among other known brand names. When it comes to your AC cable connecting from your inverter to a distribution board, the ratings you need to consider are very similar. The main difference is that AC has inductance as well as resistance, which combine to form impedance. Impedance is the same as resistance in a DC system, which is what restricts the flow of current and creates losses. It is similar to how drag creates air resistance that reduces the ability of vehicles to travel fast. Essentially, there are additional losses to consider with AC cables that aren't present in DC systems. Fortunately, these tend to be small, and you won't need to concern yourself with short cable runs.

How to Earth or Ground Your System

Another major consideration that many people neglect to address is the earthing of your solar system. Earthing, or grounding, refers to linking parts of your solar system to earth, making it safe. When it comes to earthing, one of the most important aspects to consider is known as equipotential. This means that different points have the same connection to the earth; therefore, no potential difference can exist between them, resulting in current flowing from one point to another, especially through a person. It is a critical safety feature that all electrical installations need to consider.

Picture a moment when you have touched something conductive, be it a door handle or car body, and you received a static shock. The reason for this small shock is that you have a different potential difference from the object that you touch. Many times, this is caused due to shoes that you wear which insulate you from the ground. This, combined with touching or rubbing various things, results in a buildup of charge of one type or another. The surfaces that you touch moments before a static shock are almost always neutral, at an equipotential charge as the earth. You, however, have a built-up positive or negative charge which will dissipate when you come in contact with the earth, resulting in a static shock. The purpose of equipotential earthing is to ensure that all non-live parts of an electrical system are at the same potential as earth, making them safe to touch one another. The other purpose of having equipotential earthing is that any earth fault will be detected and isolated. An earth fault means that a conductor carrying electricity has a connection to a component that should not be conducting electricity. If you have a toaster constricted by metal, then the last thing you want is for the entire toaster to become live and electrocute you if you touch it. Without equipotential earthing, you would not even realize that the toaster's body was live. With equipotential earthing and the correct earthing protection, as soon as a live wire touches the toaster's body from within, the equipotential bonding conductor leads that power to earth, resulting in a trip and isolation of electricity flowing to the toaster.

More than half of the faults that occur in electrical systems are due to earth faults or incorrect earthing, so it is a good starting point.

Consideration for Lightning Risks

Another major aspect of solar systems that you should consider is lightning protection. Lightning behaves in much the same way that static electricity behaves. There is a build up of charge between the clouds and the earth, resulting in a voltage that spirals until lightning results in a burst of current from one to the other, discharging the buildup of charge. The trouble with solar systems is that they act as a beacon for lightning. The myth that lightning strikes the highest point has some validity to it, but probably not in the way that you perceive it.

When you install your solar system, you should carry out a lightning risk assessment to know what type of protection you should install. The last thing you want is for your solar panels to be hit with a lightning strike, causing your solar system to need replacement. A typical lightning risk assessment uses the rolling sphere method to determine all the at-risk points of a lightning strike. At the end of the day, lightning is trying to reach equipotential earth. If there is an array of solar panels, then there are many areas where lightning may strike. This is where you need to install an equipotential lightning rod with its own dedicated link to earth. These lightning rods are not necessarily the massive poles that you see atop skyscrapers, but are relatively short lightning rods that are able to reduce the risk of lightning striking any one of the adjacent panels using the rolling sphere method.

Historically, lightning masts were specified according to a general rule. From the tip of the lightning rod, if you took a 45-degree angle down towards earth in all directions and drew an imaginary line down, that is the level of protection that it can offer. For example, if you had a 10 foot high lightning rod, it could only effectively protect against lightning strikes in a 10 foot radius around the rod. This method is still a good rule of thumb, but the improved method is known as the rolling sphere method. In this method, an imaginary sphere of a diameter determined by the level of protection required is rolled over your installation, and any point that it touches should be fitted with a lightning rod of a specific height. It sounds confusing, but imagine you have a beach ball and you roll it over a kitchen counter. Each point that it touches requires a lightning rod. Now imagine that a lightning rod is a mug placed where the ball first touches the counter. The beach ball now needs to roll over the mug. When the ball touches the counter again, you need another mug or lightning rod, and so on. By the end of rolling the beach ball over the counter, the mugs should prevent the ball from touching the counter altogether. This is like having lightning rods placed on a solar array. Instead of the lightning reaching your solar panels, like the beach ball not reaching the countertop, the lighting will strike the lightning rods, like the beach ball only touching the mugs.

The goal with solar systems is to have fewer lightning rods of lower height to reduce any impact from potential shading or obstructions due to having these rods stick out from your solar system. It is a cheap exercise to add these lightning arrestors, and they may well protect your panels, cables, inverter, and batteries from a catastrophic failure due to a lightning strike. Also, many insurance companies will insist that you have some form of lightning protection in order to cover your solar system or what your solar system is mounted on, such as a house. Insurance companies recognize the fire hazard that comes with a solar system, and you don't want to lose everything without any coverage.

All solar systems, especially those installed on houses, require an easily accessible kill switch. This is typically connected and mounted outside the vehicle or house so that, if there is a fire, flood, or another emergency, the solar system can be isolated from the outside without anyone having to risk their lives to go inside and risk electrocution or worse.

Specifying Your Inverter and Charge Controller

When it comes to the inverter that you select, the main criteria you need to consider is the power capacity of the inverter. If you determine that you will require 3 kW of power at any given time, you need to have an inverter to meet this demand. It is recommended that you select an inverter that is oversized for your current requirements in case you expand or need to add more load at a later stage. It is also important to figure out how many strings of solar panels can connect to your inverter. Some inverters may be rated for just a single string, while others will cater for two or three strings. This is also relevant to the system voltage of your solar system. Each panel that you add to your string will increase the DC voltage of the string. Inverters will have a maximum DC voltage rating for their input, and you cannot exceed this voltage. It would also be a waste not to make use of voltage to maximize your power generation capability. Inverters are rated with a specific power availability, and this requires both a voltage of a certain range and a current of a certain range. The best practice is to maximize your voltage as far as possible in order to get the power that you require. If the rated string voltage of an inverter is 120 Volts of DC power, then connecting a string rated at 48 Volts DC would reduce the power capability of the inverter. It is possible to expand in the future for such a consideration. Still, it would also be possible to expand the system by connecting a second string of panels in parallel to the first string that has been connected. This is typically determined by the configuration and connection of your combiner box or the rating of and number of DC inputs on your inverter.

Inverters also put out a high-pitched sound that, in some cases, falls into the audible range for humans. It's important to consult the inverter manual or, preferably, see a demo unit in action to avoid purchasing an inverter that gives off this noise, as it can be highly annoying and result in headaches over time. Most inverters will have an operational frequency rating that you can look at and compare to audible frequencies, which typically range from 20 Hertz to 20,000 Hertz for people with perfect hearing. Do not confuse this audible frequency range with the switching frequency of the semiconductive devices.

One of the most useful features of many modern-day off-grid inverters is that they are equipped with a charge controller built into the unit. This makes it a single device to connect your batteries, solar panels, and AC loads to via a DB. It makes the inverters a space and cost-saver in the long run. The inverter will be able to convert the DC power generated into AC power for your consumption when the sun is out. At the same time, the excess power generated will be used to charge your batteries via the inverter's built-in charge controller. This allows you to maximize the power that your solar panels generate and avoid wasting power. This system is streamlined since there is only one controlling device handling all the functionality. This added efficiency and quick response of the unit make it the most functional connection for inverters. Suppose your load demand is too great for your solar panels to handle. In that case, the charge controller works in the opposite direction and power is drawn from the batteries to make up the difference between the power that you generate and the power demanded by your load. This is expanded into the night when your solar panels are not generating any power, and your batteries are relied on to supply power to your loads. The change between operations is seamless and uninterrupted, so you will not even be aware of the change from solar to battery supply.

When it comes to charge controllers, many people don't understand their purpose. If batteries charge at 12 VDC, and you have a 12 VDC solar panel, why can't you just connect the one directly onto the other? The main reason for this is that batteries are sensitive to either voltage or current. Some batteries require a stable voltage level that doesn't spike too high, which could damage the battery's insulation, such as with gel-type batteries. On the other hand, some batteries cannot be charged quickly from a large current flowing through them, such as with AGM batteries. To avoid these two problems, charge controllers monitor and limit the amount of current that flows to the batteries as well as the voltage exposed to the batteries in order to charge them according to their manufacturer specifications. In this way, your batteries will experience a longer lifespan and will be suitably protected while charging and discharging.

These devices are typically connected to solar panel strings in the DC circuit. The advantage of having a charge controller on the DC circuit is that there are fewer losses than on the AC side, such as battery charger units consisting of a bidirectional rectifier and filter unit. Battery chargers that are connected to the AC circuit are more commonly seen in grid-tied solar systems, as they will charge batteries from the solar power and the grid without discerning between the two. There is no grid withh off-grid solar systems; therefore, batteries will only be charged from the solar panels. Additionally, these batteries act as the source of power when the solar panels are not generating power, so if they run out of charge, there is no power at all. This differs from grid-tied systems where the grid can still charge the batteries even if the solar panels cannot.

Solar inverters that have a built-in battery charger system are preferable to using two different devices. A lot of this has to do with the intelligence that is built into modern-day inverters. Most leading brands have what is known as a human-machine interface (HMI) touch screen and a connection to the internet. These devices often have a read-only or adjustable phone application that you can use to connect to your inverter from your phone. The displays are very useful and include total power generated by your solar panels, percentage of charge on your batteries, your load demand at any given time, and trending data for you to track your average power usage and plan better. You will also see if it makes sense to expand your solar array or battery bank based on your needs in this way.

These features are typically available for you no matter where you are, provided you have an internet connection and provided your inverter has the capability and internet connection. It is password-protected, so there is very low risk when it comes to cybersecurity. Most modern systems are equipped with a view-only mode, which allows you to see all of the settings and live data but not change anything. This secures you from someone logging into your system and reducing the efficiency or changing settings that don't work best for you. We live in the age of information, and the more data you are able to gather and observe, the easier it is to monitor, repair, or carry out maintenance on your system. If you note that the power generated by your solar panels is lower this month than the previous one, then perhaps you should clean your panels and see what impact this will have. It's also a key indicator as to how well your batteries are aging. Inverters equipped with battery charge controllers will also have basic monitoring functionality to inform you if there is a problem with your batteries. This allows you to replace or repair a battery before it fails or reaches its end of life, leaving you in a blackout situation.

Specifying Your Fuses

Another feature included in your inverter that you should look out for is having built-in fuses and surge arrestors. These devices can be installed separately and are just as effective, but it saves cost to already have these devices sized and installed internally in your inverter. Also, make sure the inverter is lightweight and easy to install. Most inverters will come with a wall mount kit that allows you to drill and mount the inverter into a wall easily. Make sure that you select the right mounting kit based on the wall type. Metal, wood, and concrete will all have slightly different mounting kits based on materials best suited to keep the inverter sturdy.

If your selected inverter is not equipped with built-in fuses, then you will have to specify and purchase them yourself. It's important to identify the areas where fuses will be most practical. If you have a distribution board on the AC side of your inverter, then all protection devices should be mounted in there. This means that you need to worry about fuses coming into your inverter from your solar panels. These fuses need to be mounted somewhere, and typically what people will do when installing fuses is to use a combiner box. A combiner box links all your strings of panels together and has fuses and surge arrestors built into it. Your solar panel string lengths and panel sizes need to be considered when specifying your fuses. The more panels you have in series, the more current will be drawn from the solar array. This is also relevant because the rated total load current of solar panels, typically at 25 degrees Celsius, or 77 degrees Fahrenheit, is less than 10% different from the solar panel fault current. Essentially, the fuse sizes have to be very precise in order to avoid blowing a fuse when the solar array is operating correctly and not having a fuse blow when there is a legitimate short circuit fault. Additionally, not all fuses are suitable to use in DC circuits, so you need to specify that the fuses will be used in a DC system and what the expected voltage will be. Fuses are typically rated for 1,000 VAC, but this would only be suitable for use in DC systems of just over 700 VDC. This is why caution is needed when choosing your solar system fuses. Suppose you have a single string of panels. In that case, you only need to refer to the maximum operating current and fault current of a single panel in order to specify your fuses for a string connected in series. If the full rated current is 9 A and the fault current is rated at 11 A, then you should ideally choose a 10 A fuse in order to protect your string from short circuits (Clifton, 2016).

Chapter 6:
Build Your Own Solar Power System

The process of taking the theory covered in the above chapters and putting it into a physical installation requires some fundamentals that are necessary to consider. This chapter will look at practical ways to purchase the right equipment, install it correctly, and prove the system works the way you designed it. As with all designs, it is always good to test the system in a simulation before you buy so you don't find that it isn't correct or as effective as you had anticipated after going out and spending the money. There are many online resources that are free of charge, and we recommend Helioscope. It is a paid software, but there is a 30 day free trial that you can make use of. In the software, you can mimic how your solar panels will be installed, specify the exact inverter and battery backup, and the software will determine how much energy you will be able to capture over the year and pick up if there is something that you have specified which simply won't work. It's safe to say that the energy output from solar panels varies from summer to winter. Surprisingly, solar panels often perform better in the winter months because many places are drier and do not experience as much rainfall or snowfall during the winter. This increases the amount of daylight sun hours per day, increasing the quantity of energy generated by the solar panels. Another point is that solar panels have a higher efficiency when kept in cooler conditions with high levels of sunlight. They typically perform best at around 20 degrees Celsius or 68 degrees Fahrenheit, but it can vary. Temperatures above 25 degrees Celsius or 77 degrees Fahrenheit result in a degradation of energy efficiency (Almerini, 2021). Because of this phenomenon, winter months often lead to more efficient solar power generation.

However, due to the reduced number of hours of sun in the sky during the day, you will likely see a drop in daylight sun hours and energy produced throughout the day. Moreover, most users have higher energy requirements in the winter months than they do in the summer months due to additional lighting and, potentially, heating devices that are used in winter. It's important to know your winter and summer power demands so that you don't size your system for one season but neglect the other. This may not be relevant to you if you are installing a solar system on a holiday home or RV, which you only make use of in the summer, but it is still an important consideration when sizing your solar system. Software such as Helioscope is user-friendly and takes you through a step-by-step guide to size your system according to the theory you have learned and highlights areas you may have missed along the way. It will automatically consider your geographical location, predict meteorological data based on historical data, and help you see what you can expect to get out of your solar system.

Building on this note, one of the first things you need to decide when installing your solar panels is to angle them to capture the most energy from the sun. The angle of the sun shifts between winter and summer. If you live in the northern hemisphere, the sun will not rise due east and set due west. Instead, it rises and sets further south, and how far south is dependent on the seasons. The sun will rise and set further south during the winter compared to the summer, which can have a massive impact on how much power you can generate. The thing to consider here is how much you should tilt your solar panels towards the south in order to capture the most sunlight possible. Of course, this is reversed in the southern hemisphere, where the sun rises and sets to the north.

It's a good idea to measure the space where you want to install your panels before you go out and purchase them. Measuring the space also involves verifying the areas that will receive sunlight throughout the day and which areas may experience shade. Consider this with the different times of the year, as a shadow may not be cast during the summer months on a certain area, but is cast in the same area during winter. It's also a good idea to decide where you wish to install your inverter, battery charger, and batteries. This will help you determine the cable route that you will take when installing your DC cables from your solar panels to your inverter. Also, consider where your existing AC DB is located if this is relevant to your installation.

If you are installing your panels on the roof of a house, what type of roofing is it? Corrugated iron and tiles require different mounting clips to secure the panels to a rigid structure, such as the roof. Also, consider that you will need to clean your solar panels at least once every few months. Installations aren't just about what is convenient for you, but also what is practical in the future, especially regarding maintenance and replacement work that you may have to carry out in the future.

Now is a good time to consider the tools that you will require for installing the solar system. For the most part, the tools are relatively simple. A multimeter of some kind is highly recommended so that you can measure each solar panel as well as voltage, earthing, and frequency in your AC circuit. It's a handy tool while installing and testing your system to prove that it is working how you designed it. You will need standard handheld tools such as screwdrivers, especially a small, flat screwdriver that is commonly called a terminal screwdriver. This tool is typically used for terminating wires in electrical installations. A socket set, spanners and Allen wrenches are useful to have, as many inverters and mounting structures will require that you have these tools.

You will also require wire cutters or side cutters in order to cut cables or wires where needed. If you are using a larger cable with armoring, you may require a knife such as a Stanley knife to cut through the cable's outer sheath before stripping the armoring. It is useful to have a long nose and standard pliers for this purpose as well. Wire strippers are useful to strip the insulation off the ends of wires off to mount a connector clip, lug, or bootlace in order to connect the wire to a terminal of some kind. If you do not have wire strippers, it is possible to strip wires with side cutters or wire cutters.

The next tool is essential for electrical installations, and that is a crimping tool. This tool is used to crimp the wire with a lug, bootlace, or connector clip. In almost all electrical installations, these terminations are used instead of using bare copper or aluminum.

There may be an additional need to have some power tools handy. It is ideal to use battery-powered tools, as they are more practical with installations such as solar systems. A battery-powered drill and angle grinder should be suitable to cater to all of your power tool needs.

The method for installing your solar panels is quite straightforward once you can identify the surface you are installing. A rooftop mounted solar system will vary from a ground-mounted system or a flush-mounted system on an RV or boat. Some cabins do not have a tilt angle that benefits from angling it towards the sun. In order to mount the panels so that they can capture as much power from sun up to sundown, it may be more practical to build a mounting structure to maximize the panels' alignment with the sun, which involves using, preferably, an aluminum frame.

Something that many people neglect to do when it comes to installing their solar system or carrying out any project that requires you to do it yourself is to choose and learn how to use your tools correctly. It may seem very straightforward to crimp a lug onto a wire using a wire crimping tool, but many people will do it incorrectly. Even electricians often fail to follow best practices when making use of handheld tools. This results in poor workmanship and faults that would have been easily avoided if the installers had used their tools correctly. The more you use your tools, the more using them becomes second nature to you, but the first few times you use a new tool may feel unusual.

This goes for all the simple tools that are required for this installation. When stripping the insulation material off of wires using wire strippers or side cutters, be sure to strip off the right amount for the lug, clip, or bootlace that you intend to fasten onto the wire. Lugs require a short section of approximately 1 cm, or 0.4 inches, of the conductor (typically copper) to be exposed on your wire. Next up is to put the lug over the wire with the clamp section over the live conductor and the insulated section over the wire's insulation. You also need to make sure that you crimp the lug on the right way around. When a lug is crimped, there should be no copper or live conductor strands sticking out on the live connection part of the lug. The insulated part of the lug should also have a snug fit over the wire conductor without any live parts of the wire being exposed here. You can test how well a wire is crimped by pulling on it to confirm that it won't slip off the wire at any point.

This is just an example of how to use one of the handheld tools that many people aren't familiar with. There are many resources, including YouTube or even the supplier of the tools, that you can go to in order to learn good tool work practices. This preparation and learning activity may seem trivial, but it is a useful skill to have for any DIY project moving forward.

All new installations that you make to your home or vehicle are based on international or local standards. There are wiring standards, sizing standards, and aspects that will directly affect your solar installation. There is a good chance that these standards will not directly impact you in going off-grid, but there is a reason that they have been drafted, and you should not ignore them. It encompasses every small detail that you can possibly consider in your system, from the inverter you select, to earthing and safety requirements, to the mechanical reliability of your structures. Building a solar system that adheres to international standards means that you will automatically install a legal, ethical system and fits your requirements as need be.

RV Mounted Solar System

When it comes to RV solar systems, you want to mount your panels straight to the RV roof to reduce any drag you might experience while driving. It is possible to mount a rooftop system that is adjustable once you are parked to absorb more sunlight, but this may not be the best option. It has a higher initial capital cost and means that you have moving components that may require replacing. It also means that you have to get up onto the roof to adjust the angle every time you stop, which isn't a practical option. It also means that you need to ensure that the solar panels are flush and secure when you wish to drive again.

A simpler solution is going with a rooftop mount system that is flexible and does not adjust. You also don't want to drill too many holes in the roof to reduce the risk of leaking. There are great sealants available on the market that prevent leaking, but they are less effective than a system that does not require drilling to mount solar panels. There is the option of using double-sided tape that is highly resilient to environmental conditions and will adequately secure your solar panels to the roof. One such type of double-sided tape is very high bond (VHB) tape. It varies in length and width, but a good option from a reliable manufacturer to use when mounting your panels to the roof would be 3M 4941 VHB tape (Dennis, 2019). This tape is very durable and is very good at maintaining its adhesive properties even with large temperature fluctuations. When applying this tape, the surface that you mount it to must be clean. Making use of alcohol or methylated spirits even after washing the surface clean is a good idea. This will reduce the risk of dust or particles getting caught in the area that you will stick the solar panels to. The disadvantage of using this type of tape over using a drill and mount system is that you will have difficulty removing the panel at a later stage if you wish to remove or replace it.

If this is a concern that you have, then opt for drilling and tapping with a flush mount kit for the solar panels of your choice. You will have to add sealant around each area you have drilled and test that the sealant works effectively. Self-leveling sealant is readily available and will be required for the DC wires to be installed from the solar panels outside the RV to the inverter, batteries, and charge controller system on the inside.

Boat Mounted Solar System

A boat-mounted system has a lot of similarities to RV-mounted systems. The main thing to consider with a boat-mounted system is that there is a lot of moisture. The panels and outside will almost certainly get wet with saltwater rather than just rainwater (depending on whether you have a freshwater or saltwater application in mind). Corrosion at sea level is notoriously bad, and this factor shouldn't be ignored with your solar system either. Fortunately, solar panels and solar wire connectors (typically MC4 connectors) are rated to handle this type of environment. It is still good practice to clean your solar panels with fresh water frequently, just as you would the rest of the deck on any boat. Soap water and clean freshwater are all that you need.

It's also of note to point out that, in a boat installation, there is a lot of movement on deck, and the movement of a boat results in a lot more impact style motion compared to driving on the road in an RV installation. This could result in areas that have been sealed being weakened or cracked over time, which could lead to a leak from the exterior to the interior of the hull. In order to prevent this from occurring, you should use high-quality sealant that is rated for marine applications. These are readily available from hardware stores, and this is an area where you shouldn't worry about cost-saving and should focus on purchasing a high-quality product. It's also advisable that you buy excess sealant to have on hand in the future in case you have any issues with leaking due to natural wear and tear.

Small Home or Cabin Mounted Solar System

This type of installation is almost always going to be made up of rigid solar panels. The system is non-mobile; therefore, the weight and air resistance would not be as much of a factor as with RV's, boats, and other mobile solar systems. A word of caution here is to confirm that you will not compromise the integrity of the existing structure where you mount the panels. Whether big or small, all cabins and houses are designed to carry a certain weight on them. This usually takes into consideration various roofing tiles and extreme weather conditions that exert additional force on them. They also cater to water or snow build-up, and even the weight of a person walking over them. Now, add the weight of a dozen or so solar panels, each weighing around 20 kilograms, or 44 pounds, then add frames, wires, lightning rods, and all additional support brackets that may be required. This could add as much as 300 kilograms, or 660 pounds, of additional weight on top of your roof, which is a large additional weight. The last thing that you want is to have your roof collapse when you go up to clean your panels or have the panels act as a sail in the event of high wind, ripping them off of your roof.

It's also important to consider your access to running water, particularly with enough pressure to clean solar panels mounted on top of the roof of a structure. Running water is ideal to use in order to clean your panels. You also need to consider having a ladder to easily gain access to the panels in order to clean them. Additionally, mounting the panels on top of roof tiling or corrugated iron requires mounting, which may compromise the waterproofing of your roof. Be sure to test that you have adequately sealed the roof after you have mounted the panels before experiencing rainfall. Take care when determining your cable route when taking the DC wires from the solar panel strings to the location in your home where you have decided to mount the solar inverter, preferably close to the DB. The shorter your cable length is, the fewer losses you will experience, and the less cable you will have to purchase. This doesn't mean that you should run a direct line from one point to another, as there may be obstacles in the way. You want your cable runs to be neat and not to take away from the aesthetic of your home. You may want to install the cables in skirting or cable trunking. You can run the wires above the ceiling, then drill through the ceiling and run the wires down to the inverter. In this way, you will only have to worry about sealing this point in the roof down to the inverter. It will also avoid having the eyesore of wires running through your living space.

Don't forget to keep vermin out of the areas where electrical wires will be located. Rats and other rodents are nasty with this, as they will eat their way through the insulation of your wiring and cause a short circuit and loss of ability to generate power. Make use of flame retardant foam where necessary to keep vermin out and remove the fire hazard that comes with using regular sealant spray foam.

Solar systems on any home can drive up the property value substantially. However, this does also come with additional expenses when it comes to home insurance policies. These premiums will inevitably go up due to the addition of a solar system on the roof. It may also impact your property tax rates, depending on the country, state, or county you live in.

Connection Methods

The most common method of connecting your solar system is to have your solar panels and batteries connected to your charge controller. A typical charge controller and inverter will have connection diagrams that the manufacturer provides. There will generally be more than one option, but there will always be a recommended setup that matches your requirement.

The most common connection between the primary components is having a common negative terminal between the battery charger, solar panels, and batteries. In DC circuits, you always want to have the same reference voltage. In many installations, this negative terminal of a DC circuit is earthed, such as in cars. However, in solar systems, it is highly recommended that the negatives are not earthed. There are circumstances where this is required, but a good rule of thumb is to leave the negative terminal floating unless the manufacturer explicitly recommends that you earth them. The term "floating" is used to describe a point that may be earthed but is intentionally left without an earth reference point.

The inverter will have a positive and negative input from the batteries as well as a bypass connection from the charge controller, typically on the positive input. The charge controller controls this bypass connection. When the batteries are fully charged, excess power is bypassed from the batteries and connected directly to the inverter.

The inverter will then have a connection on the AC side to your load via a DB. This connection is via an AC cable. There is typically an isolation and protection device in the DB that acts as an incomer. The solar panel power is an incoming power to be distributed to where you require it.

Some inverters directly input from the batteries with a built-in charge controller and a direct connection to the solar panels. These units typically have no maximum power point tracker (MPPT) connections or a built-in MPPT connection. Other solar inverters have input from solar panels via an external MPPT. An MPPT is essentially a converter device that optimizes the balance between the DC voltage of the solar panels, your battery bank, and your AC system. It is beneficial to have more than one MPPT device built into your solar inverter or housed externally. Two separate units can monitor and optimize the power generated by solar panels oriented in different ways without incurring losses across your whole solar array.

When you hook your battery system up, you need to refer to the voltage rating of the charge controller and solar inverter battery input. Many of the products available on the market are limited to 12 V or 24 V, so connecting your batteries in a 48 V configuration is not a viable option. Suppose you were to connect a series of batteries resulting in a 48 V configuration to an MPPT or inverter input that is only rated for 24 V. In that case, you will damage the insulation and other electronics inside the device. Fortunately, most devices have built-in over-voltage protection, which will blow in a similar way to a fuse if the voltage level exceeds the rated voltage. These components, known as metal oxide varistors (MOVs), will have to be replaced if they are damaged in this way, and your device will not be able to operate until this is done.

You have two options when connecting multiple batteries: Connect them in either a series or parallel configuration. If you connect them in series, their voltage will increase, whereas when you connect them in parallel, their voltage will remain the same. The power goes up with the same proportions in both cases. In the case of a parallel connection, the current, or amps, supplied doubles instead of the voltage. It is always recommended that you use an even number of batteries and match your connections throughout. If you want to make up a 24 V battery setup, it isn't good practice to use three 12 V batteries. Suppose you were to put two batteries in parallel and connect these two in series with one more battery. In that case, you will be able to achieve your overall 24 V system. Still, the battery alone will have a lot more current flowing through it, which typically leads to heating issues, charging problems, and a reduction in the battery lifespan.

Ensure that the wires you use to connect your batteries are thick enough to handle the current that will flow through them. It is common practice to clamp lugs onto these fairly thick wires and add heat shrink wrap to maintain the insulation and avoid flashovers of any kind. Heat shrink is an insulating material, similar to insulation tape, but it does not use glue or other adhesives that wear over time. The heat shrink wrap is placed over the point where the lug and wire connect, and when heat is applied, the insulation material shrinks to fit snugly over the connection point.

It's also good practice to install a fuse, or DC-rated circuit breaker between your DC devices. This implies that you require a DC circuit breaker or DC-rated fuse in your connections between your battery charge controller and batteries and between your batteries and your inverter battery inputs. The added benefit of having these devices is that they can act as safety isolation devices if you need to do any maintenance or replacement work on your DC system. When working on your batteries, you should turn the circuit breaker off or open the circuit using the circuit breakers between the batteries and charge controller and between the batteries and inverter before you work on them. This will reduce any risk of electrocution or injury from the batteries discharging through you when working on them.

This can be expanded into protection or isolation devices on the output of your inverter. All DBs that feed your loads should have their own protection devices, such as fuses or circuit breakers. Circuit breakers are the preferred method in these installations as they can be reset and used for up to 10,000 operations. In comparison, a fuse will operate once and burn out, requiring replacement. Fuses respond quicker than any other protection device, but a circuit breaker is preferable in the case of small household loads, even though it takes between three and five times as long to trip. Fuses will blow within 20 milliseconds of a major short circuit, whereas circuit breakers will typically trip after around 100 milliseconds. This doesn't add a significant amount of risk for small power systems, such as homes, RV's, and other small-scale solar systems.

Chapter 7:
Blueprints And Equations

In order to fully understand and implement the theory introduced above, you will need some common equations to calculate your requirements. The last thing you want is to undersize your solar system and be left in blackout scenarios on a frequent basis. It's also detrimental to oversize your solar system and end up paying excessive amounts for a system that you don't fully utilize. If your system can handle a house, but you only require it for your RV on weekend getaways, then you may have oversized your system. This is commonly referred to as an overdesign. There is nothing inherently wrong with overdesigning your solar system, only that you will end up paying more for the system than required without reaching a return on investment for the system.

When calculating the size of your solar system, you need to look at the loads that you will supply with it. Now is the time to look at the power or current requirements of the combined loads and determine how often the loads will be connected and how much power they will draw at any given time. If you are supplying three sockets rated for 15 amps, it doesn't mean that you will be using 15 amps 24 hours per day. The two factors that you need to look at are the frequency of using loads and how much of the loads will be used at any given time. With a 15 A socket outlet, you may be using 10 A, so you would be oversizing your solar system to cater for this. In the same way, you could size your backup battery storage to supply these loads for 24 hours of the day only to realize later that a lot of loads will be for things that only draw power for half of the time.

Let's start by looking at how many batteries you require for your needs. We will also consider how many solar panels you require and the type of inverter you require. The best inverters on the market have a battery charger module installed in them, as discussed in Chapter 5. These units typically have more than one MPPT to connect strings of panels angled in different ways to maximize the peak sun hours of different seasons. That being said, you need to know what is required from an inverter as well as its efficiency. Furthermore, there are things that manufacturers and distributors typically wouldn't disclose to an end-user that will be discussed in this chapter. An end-user is the description that manufacturers use to describe a person or company that will use their products. This separates them from distributors or stockholders who sell the products on behalf of the manufacturer. The ratings that manufacturers display on their datasheets are legitimate but are often based on ideal circumstances. In reality, some losses are taken that decrease the efficiency of products, but most manufacturers do not elaborate on this in detail, as it shows the limitations of their product. This is not openly displayed by competitors either.

A typical small home with two bedrooms and two bathrooms will require about eight sockets. Assuming each socket is rated at 5 amperes, there will be a total available capacity of 40 amps. That being said, it is not as though you will require a full 40 amps at 110 VAC throughout the day. Some loads will only be needed through the night, such as lights. Some loads will only be needed when you engage the load, such as swimming pool pumps. You need to consider your coincidence factor. This relates to how often loads are on. It's perfectly fine to consider your microwave when sizing your solar system, but, realistically, how often is your microwave running? This is a simplified definition of the load factor of a system. This is also why the main incoming circuit breaker from the utility is sized smaller than the addition of all the feeder breakers to household loads. You do not have everything running simultaneously and do not use the amount of electricity that you may believe that you do at any given point in time.

This coincidence factor is defined by how often you have your loads running on an average basis, and you should always cater to a worst-case scenario when you run loads more often than usual. It is basically figuring out how often your loads will run together because loads running together will draw a large amount of power. If you have a 15 A socket and three loads that require 5 A each, how often will you run these three loads together? It's like running your fridge, toaster, and microwave at the same time. This would be a highly unusual scenario, so perhaps you would only ever run two out of these three loads at any given time. What these two fundamentals translate to is that you may have a 15 A socket but will probably only ever have a maximum of 10 A being used 10% of the time, and it may only run 5 A the other 90% of the time. This can help you in specifying your battery storage requirements. In order to calculate your battery size from your current or power requirement, you need to make use of the following equations:

Power (W) = Current (A) x Voltage (V)

Energy (Wh) = Power (W) x Time (Hours)

Battery demand (Ah) = Energy (Wh) / Battery voltage (V)

Battery size (Ah) = Battery Demand (Ah) / Depth of Discharge (%)

Number of batteries = Battery size (Ah) / Single Battery size available (Ah)

Basically, if you wish to power a socket rated for 15 A at a 10 A level for a 12 hour period, then the battery size you require can be calculated in the following way:

Power = current (10 A) x voltage (110 V, the standard voltage in the US)

Power = 10 x 110 = 1,150 W

Energy = 1,150 W x 12 hours = 13,800 Wh

Battery demand (Ah) = Energy (Wh) / AC Voltage (VAC) = 13,800 Wh / 12 V = 1,150 Ah

Now, let's assume that the battery that you wish to select has a depth of discharge of 60%:

Battery size (Ah) = Battery total rating (Ah) / Depth of discharge (%) = 1,150 Ah / 0.6 = 1,917 Ah

Next, you need to take into consideration a battery rating that you may have selected. The battery datasheet will provide you with the Ah rating as well as the depth of discharge. Assume you wish to use 200 Ah batteries and that the 60% depth of discharge used above is in line with the batteries' capability:

Number of batteries = Battery requirement (Ah) / Battery rating (Ah) = 1,1917 Ah / 200 Ah = 9.5 (round up to 10 batteries)

This doesn't consider your coincidence and load factors, which will decrease the number of batteries that you require considerably. Let's say that you wish to have power available for your 15 A socket but will only use a 5 A load for a total of 24 hours to power a fridge. Let's say that you have an additional two 2 A loads that you will only use half of the time. Let's assume one of these is to feed your lights, and the other is to power electronics to charge your phone and other devices. This means that your coincidence factor is 1 for the 5 A fridge load and 0.5 for the 2 A light and charger loads. Now, to determine your coincidence factor, you must consider how often the loads will run simultaneously. As we have mentioned, the fridge will run the entire time, coinciding with both the other loads. However, how often will you run the lights and charging devices together? Most likely, only at night when you require the lights, so you can assume a coincidence factor of 0.75. This means that three-quarters of the time that these devices operate, they will be operating simultaneously. Your overall load demand changes substantially because of this and can be worked out as a percentage of the original 10 A that you had planned for using the following simplified weighted equations:

Load Demand (A) x Load factor (%) x Coincidence Factor (%) = Actual Demand (A)

This can be used to calculate each contributing load and added together to come to a weighted average. In this example, we have three loads to consider as follows:

1. Fridge Load Demand (10 Amps) x Load Factor (1.0) x Coincidence Factor (1.0) = Actual Fridge Demand (5 Amps)

2. Light Load Demand (2 Amps) x Load Factor (0.5) x Coincidence Factor (0.75) = Actual Light Demand (0.75 Amps)

3. Charger Load Demand (2 Amps) x Load Factor (0.5) x Coincidence Factor (0.75) = Actual Charger Demand (0.75 Amps)

Total of the Actual Demand Loads = 5 Amps + 0.75 Amps + 0.75 Amps = 6.5 Amps

This is essentially 65% of the size you had catered for, meaning that the 10 batteries you initially thought you would require could be reduced to eight units, as an even number of batteries is ideal.

This is just a simple rule of thumb method to calculate the basics without considering all the complex factors that can go with it. This rule of thumb calculates how many batteries and panels are required, what your cable size should be, and what inverter rating you need is accurate by over 95%, so it's a good starting point for your system (Energy Matters, n.d.). You may go through a few more iterations of your design after the first one. This is particularly true if the original cost is very high or if the inverters, batteries, and panels on the market don't accurately match your design. You may also find that you hadn't considered a factor, such as the DC voltage of your strings, and that changes your entire design.

One of the most important aspects to consider with your solar system is weight. This is especially true for a system mounted on the roof of a house or a structure, such as an RV. Most vehicles will be constructed with a chassis or body that can support additional weight but may completely alter gravity. With any moving body, the center of gravity completely alters the handling of a vehicle. Turning will be more sluggish, and the risk of rolling or suffering from understeer is a major concern. Understeer is when you turn the vehicle, but it feels as though it has a delay and pulls you toward the straight line of your trajectory for your approach to a turn.

For non-mobile installations, the primary concern is the structural integrity of the installation. If you have a rooftop that was constructed to hold roof tiles only, and you feel as though you cannot walk on the roof to inspect it because it is creaking under your weight, then the chances of that same roof being able to support several solar panels are next to nothing. Each individual solar panel that is 2 m by 1 m, or 3 ft by 6 ft, weighs roughly 20 kilograms, or 45 pounds, excluding the mounting structure and equipment required for it. This is not considering the additional force experienced from wind, rain, hail, snow, or any other weather condition.

You must be aware of the structure you will mount your solar panels on, where the points of reinforcement are, and how it may affect your property or vehicle insurance. Again, it is essential to highlight the kill switch and minuscule increase in fire risk of a solar system in any installation to keep a low insurance premium on your asset. When sizing your load requirements, it is best to look at your structure and determine the weight capacity of the existing structure. It isn't much of a concern for RVs or boats, as they can handle the additional weight on top of the main chassis. When it comes to cabins and tiny houses, the roofs may not be able to handle an additional 300 kgs or 700 pounds. Be cautious in these scenarios, as a roof may be able to take this additional weight as a static object, but that does not mean that it can handle this additional weight in a thunderstorm or if there is a significant amount of wind or snow. It may also result in an insurance nightmare where a roof was designed on standard applications of handling weather effects, and now you are adding another component to this. It's always a good idea to look at the building blueprints to see the size and weight capacity of the roof before installing your solar system. It's also valuable in this instance to enquire what the implications would be. It's not worth it to add your solar system only for a terrible occurrence, such as a natural disaster, to happen, and insurance companies refuse to cover the damage because of the addition of a solar system.

When sizing the required load of your system, particularly a house system, the best way to determine an accurate requirement is to look at your existing utility bill. The monthly bill that you are provided based on your energy meter readings is typically determined in kWh. With this reference, you should be able to average out your annual requirements for any home or holiday home application. If you are using an average of 10 kWh per day, you will be able to size your entire system based on this, including losses due to efficiency. All solar systems experience inefficiency, and you have to cater to unexpected weather conditions which may hinder your system's ability to generate power due to overcast weather or an unusually long period where your energy demands are far higher than usual.

To do this, take your monthly average utility bill over 12 months. Then take this value and divide it by an average of

30 days to get your daily energy usage. Let's say that this value comes to 5 units, or kWh, per day for a small home. This amounts to average daily usage. In order to determine your inverter size, number and size of solar panels, and number and size of batteries, you should use similar calculations used above. The primary difference is that all power used needs to be generated by the solar panels themselves. So, take your 5 kWh per day, cater to your efficiency losses, and allow a 25% safety factor.

A safety factor is an engineering term used in situations where you need to overcompensate because too many variables are unaccounted for and cannot be accurately calculated or predicted. The weather falls under this category, which is why your safety factor is required to be so substantial. Considering this, you need to allow for flexibility to cater for 7.5 kWh per day on average. Including efficiency from your DC system to your AC system requires you to implement the following calculation:

Solar Power requirement (DC kWh) = Power Demand (AC kWh) / Predicted overall efficiency (%)

Power Requirement = 7.5 kWh / 0.85 = 8.83 kWh per day. Average this up to 9 kWhdc per day.

This amount of power per day requires that you have solar panels that can provide this power in just the number of PSH per day. So, if you require 9 kWh in the space of 24 hours, then your solar panels need to generate at least this amount while the sun is up. Let's use the annual average for the sun being out and calculate PSH to be 7 hours per day. This necessitates that the DC system and solar system demand is as follows:

Solar DC demand (kW) = Calculated Demand (kWhdc) / Peak Sun Hours (Hours)

Solar demand (kW) = 9 / 7 = 1.28 kW

Now take this value and consider that days of overcast weather or reduced sun content result in a lack of generation ability from your solar panels. This can be averaged over the space of a year when considering the number of days of sun and the number of days of overcast weather. Let's assume a situation where the sun is only expected to shine for half of the year. This equates to a safety factor of two in order to ensure that you can generate enough power in a single sunny day to last over two days without any other form of power generation.

Solar Supply (kW) = Solar demand (kW) x (Days of sunlight per year / Total days per year)

Solar supply = 1.28kW x (182.5/365) = 2.6 kW

Now, this is starting to line up to a solar array size in a more understandable manner. It would be best to look at the solar panel sizes available on the market for your usage and allow yourself to generate enough power for your current system while allowing for future expansion. It is advisable to size your solar panels to cater to this demand with one additional panel and size your battery system and inverter for 1.5 times.

If you use 360 W solar panels, as 360 W and 320 W solar panels are most readily available, then you will require:

Number of panels = Power demand (kW) / Solar panel size (kW)

Number of panels = 2.6 / 0.4 = 6.5 panels

For this requirement, seven solar panels sized at 400 W or eight panels rated at 360 W should be enough for this system. Determining the number of panels that you require is the first step to take.

The next thing that you should determine is how you will hook up your solar panels. Let's take the typical example covered above, where a 360W solar panel is selected. Will you connect these eight panels in series to form a single string, which is possible to do? To calculate if this is possible, you need to find the voltage of the solar panels by referring to their datasheet. Most datasheets will list the operational voltage as Vmax or Vmp. This is the maximum operating voltage of each solar system, assuming ideal conditions of high solar irradiance and a temperature lower than 25 degrees Celsius, or 77 degrees Fahrenheit. This is not to be mistaken with Voc, which is also typically listed on solar panel datasheets. These values are when the solar panels are open-circuited or not connected to an inverter, with no current flowing through them.

When you connect solar panels in series, you add their voltage in order to get the total voltage. It is the same concept as connecting batteries together in series, with each battery adding to the overall system voltage across all the batteries. Let's use a typical voltage rating for a single 360 W CanadianSolar solar panel at 45 Volts to continue the example used above. To calculate your entire string voltage, use the following equation:

String Voltage (VDC) = Individual Panel Voltage (VDC) x Number of Panels (per unit)

String Voltage (VDC) = 45 VDC x 8 panels = 360 VDC

Now that you have the string voltage, you can specify an inverter based on the power output requirements and input voltage requirements. Most single-phase inverters rated for approximately 5 kW will handle 360 VDC as the solar array input voltage.

It's always good practice to slightly oversize your solar inverter to cater to expanding your solar array size. If you mount these eight panels now, but you realize that you require more power in five years, you want to add more panels rather than have to replace your inverter for a larger unit completely.

One of the biggest disadvantages of going with a built-in charge controller unit versus a separate unit is that, if the unit fails or you are having trouble with it, you will need to replace your entire inverter, or at the very least have the entire system offline until maintenance or repair work is carried out. Compare this to a separate charge controller, which could be disconnected and replaced at a much lower cost. Many charge controllers are manufactured to work alongside a specific solar inverter, so be sure to pay attention to which units are compatible with one another. An excellent strategy to follow is to stick to the same brand to ensure that connectivity and interconnection of control and monitoring are compatible. If you decide to use a Sunny Boy inverter, try to combine it with a Sunny Boy battery charger. Likewise, if you select a Victron solar inverter, a solar charge controller and MPPT module will work best in conjunction with this product. This is also true for warranty purposes. One manufacturer providing all the devices will make it more straightforward to identify problems, rectify them, and have replacement components sent from the manufacturer without warranty claim issues.

Conclusion

The information that you have gathered throughout this book should enable you to go out there and purchase and install your first solar system. It may have seemed daunting at first, but it is very doable when you break down the overall design into smaller, more manageable tasks. It would be best to look at what you want to get out of the solar system and determine the specific area to install the solar system. It may be on an RV, a tiny house, a boat, or even a trailer. There are so many applications for solar systems, and being able to generate your own electricity, even in remote areas, without having to burn fuel, such as with a generator, is such a valuable asset to have.

Once you have determined your specific application, you need to know some of the general terms of electricity, specifically related to solar panels. You need to have a basic understanding of your voltage, current, and power, as well as the differences between AC and DC power. Another valuable bit of knowledge is in the components themselves, including protection, earthing, inverters, and cables. There is no point in going ahead and installing your own solar system if you have no idea what the different components do and the basics of how they work. The better you understand your system, the more empowered you will be to maintain or repair the system if it stops functioning the way it is supposed to. It's also crucial to have this knowledge so that you can remain safe from harm, especially from electrocution. Suppose you want to follow quality and safety standards, especially when you install, test, or do maintenance on your solar system. In that case, you should have a solar system that meets all international standards.

When selecting your batteries, it is crucial to know the difference between the various batteries on the market. You won't want to purchase liquid lead acid batteries if an AGM battery works far better for your particular requirements. You also need to know what to look out for in batteries, including their voltage, amp hour rating, physical size, depth of discharge, and all the other pros and cons associated with each battery. When confronted with several options, you need to look at what will work best for you and offer you backup power when you need it rather than run out of energy in the middle of the night, leaving you in a blackout situation. Make sure you store your batteries in a suitable location, carry out maintenance if and when necessary, connect your batteries correctly to the charge controller, inverter, or battery charger, and don't overwork your batteries and end up reducing their life span by several years. You also need to be fully conscious of your budget and how much you are willing to spend, as well as how often you will make use of your batteries. If you spend more on a high-end battery, it will last you far longer and, possibly, save you more money in the long run.

Once you have selected a suitable battery type, you need to look at the solar panels you wish to invest in. These components, along with the inverter, will be the three most significant expenses of any solar system. Choosing the right type of solar panel for yourself is also based on your application and what you hope to get out of the system. Flexible solar panels may be more suitable for vehicles, such as RV's and boats, whereas rigid panels may be more suitable for houses. You may also want to consider monocrystalline panels if you don't have a lot of physical space but want to maximize the solar system's energy output. If this isn't as important as the cost for you, then a polycrystalline panel option may be best suited to fit your needs. Keep an eye out for panels built to international standards of safety and quality, and try to choose panels with a higher energy output to get the most power out of the fewest number of panels.

You also need to decide how you want to connect your panels. There is a limit to the number of panels that you can connect in series, and the solar inverter that you connect will also have a restriction on the number of strings and combined voltage of a string, so be sure not to exceed these limitations. It's always an option to purchase a few panels to install now and expand your system at a later stage. It's also important to note that you don't necessarily need to have a large number of panels if you have a backup battery system. If you can keep the batteries fully charged when the sun is out throughout the day, why add more panels only to waste the excess power?

Now that you have your batteries and solar panels selected, you need to look at the type and size of the inverter that you need. You may require having more than one MPPT on your inverter to capture the early morning and late afternoon sun more effectively. This is a great feature, as it allows you to connect two or more strings to separate inputs and maximizes your power generation capabilities throughout the day. It's an ideal way to do this without the expense of a tracking system, where the solar panels track the sun in the sky throughout the day. Another important consideration when selecting your inverter is confirming the efficiency, installation requirements, environmental rating (especially the operational temperature range), and power rating. You have to ensure that the inverter you select is large enough to handle the amount of power generated from your solar panels and convert that DC power to more usable AC power without significant losses.

When specifying inverters, a final note is that you should save in cost and space if you find a product that already has a built-in charge controller and connection for batteries. In this way, you will have a central unit that handles your solar panels, battery charging, and discharging and supplies AC power per your demand. Several major manufacturers produce inverters like this. Although they may be more expensive, they are worth investing in, as they are typically cheaper than purchasing both an inverter and a charge controller.

Now that you have all the major components for your solar system, you need to ensure that you have all the correct tools and equipment to mount your solar panels in your designated area safely. Do not forget that solar panels generate a voltage as soon as they are exposed to sunlight, so care must be taken when connecting the solar panels in a string and to the inverter. Electrocution from the panels themselves may not be lethal, but there are major risks, given you may be working at height and could potentially fall after being shocked.

Most tools that are required are typical electrician tools. You need a crimping tool, multimeter, screwdrivers, spanners, Allen wrenches, wire strippers, and a clamp meter for all installation and functional test work. Sometimes, if you are building a frame or mounting solar panels to an RV or boat roof, you will require some power tools, including a drill and angle grinder. It is advisable to use battery-operated power tools to have them handy in any location.

Take care to follow all manufacturer specifications when carrying out the installation. If the inverter installation guide informs you that the inverter must be installed in an upright position, then you must follow this guideline. This is especially relevant when it comes to battery storage. Great care must be taken to store batteries safely.

You now have all the basic knowledge to put together your very own solar system! As you can now see, it isn't overly complicated to follow the basic steps in specifying the major components that are best suited to your needs. You also understand the basic practices for installing your solar system safely and sticking to quality and safety standards in your installation. You now are also more knowledgeable than the average person and will be able to tell if a salesperson is pushing his product on you or is trying to find the right product for your requirements, which enables you to avoid buying unnecessary components and missing out on buying parts with significant value to you.

Building your own solar setup is very rewarding and will allow you to save on electricity costs in the long run. It will enable you to use your own power and know exactly where that power came from. Whether your system is mobile or non-mobile, you will be able to generate electricity to use from the sun, will not be impacted by problems on the grid, such as blackout scenarios, and will benefit on a monetary level in the long run. This is an investment and should be viewed as the valuable asset that it is. This is also a way for you to reduce your carbon footprint and ensure that the power you use has been generated from a renewable source. We at Small Footprint Press recognize the importance of reducing our carbon footprint to live more sustainably in the twenty-first century. Every bit counts and every individual who takes the initiative to be more conscious of their impact on the environment has the ability to make a difference. If we all make these changes in our lifestyle, we will continue to thrive and avoid damaging the environment globally. You can make a difference, and if everyone realized that their efforts and contributions made an impact, then millions more would be more proactive in reducing their carbon footprint.

You can now go out and start creating your own system. There is nothing to lose in designing and pricing your system and working out the buy-back period of the system to start you off. There is no rush, and it is better to be thorough and do things right the first time than having to make changes later, which could be time-consuming or expensive. Get your design ready, then check on the various products available to you on the market today. Look out for specials and deals to maximize your cost-saving. Once you have installed your system and have it up and running, you will wonder how you ever operated without it before!

References

Almerini, A. (2021, March 5). *Everything you need to know about installing solar panels on boats.* Solar reviews. https://www.solarreviews.com/blog/solar-panels-for-boats

Crown Battery. (2018, April 24). *What is a deep cycle battery?* https://www.crownbattery.com/news/what-is-a-deep-cycle-battery-

Clifton, S. (2016, October 5). *How to fuse your solar system.* Renogy United States.

https://www.renogy.com/blog/how-to-fuse-your-solar-system/

De Rooij, D. (2020, July 27). *Solar panel angle: How to calculate solar panel tilt angle?* Sinovoltaics - Zero risk SolarTM. https://sinovoltaics.com/learning-center/system-design/solar-panel-angle-tilt-calculation/

Dennis, R. (2019, December 20). *How to install a solar panel system on your RV roof.* RV mods - RV guides - RV tips | DoItYourselfRV. https://www.doityourselfrv.com/solar-power-4/

Energy Matters. (n.d.). *Deep cycle battery guide.* https://www.energymatters.com.au/components/batteries/#battery-explanation

Enphase. (n.d.). *What is the difference between a watt and a watt-hour?* https://enphase.com/en-us/support/what-difference-between-watt-and-watt-hour

Going Solar. (2019, March 28). *How are solar panels attached to your roof? Solar panel installation.* https://goingsolar.com/how-are-solar-panels-attached-to-your-roof-solar-panel-installation/

GridFree. (2019, August 12). *Off-grid basics - Solar power systems 102.* https://gridfree.store/blogs/how-to-articles/off-grid-basics-solar-power-systems-101

Hutchison, D., & Galiardi, S. (2019, February 21). *How solar panels work: breaking it down for beginners.* Renogy United States. https://www.renogy.com/blog/how-solar-panels-work-breaking-it-down-for-beginners/

Marsh, J. (2019, January 19). *What is solar energy?* EnergySage. https://news.energysage.com/what-is-solar-energy/

Matasci, S. (2019, January 29). *Ground mount solar panels: Top 3 things you need to know.* EnergySage. https://news.energysage.com/ground-mounted-solar-panels-top-3-things-you-need-to-know/

Proinso. (2020, May 23). *8 steps to building a DIY off-grid solar system.* https://www.proinso.net/blogs/build-diy-off-grid-solar-system/

Prowse Publications LLC. (n.d. a). *Large RV solar power blueprints*. Mobile solar power made easy. https://www.mobile-solarpower.com/the-off-grid-king-power-anything.html

Prowse Publications LLC. (n.d. b). *RV solar power blueprints*. Mobile solar power made easy. https://www.mobile-solarpower.com/the-classic-400-watt-rvs-vans-buses.html

Prowse Publications LLC. (n.d. c). *Tools*. Mobile solar power made easy. https://www.mobile-solarpower.com/tools.html

Prowse Publications LLC. (n.d. d). *Van Dweller solar power blueprints*. Mobile solar power made easy. https://www.mobile-solarpower.com/the-minimalist-great-for-small-vans-and-cars.html

ShopSolarKits.com. (n.d.). *Solar load calculator | How much solar do I need?* https://shopsolarkits.com/pages/watt-hour-calculator

Solar 4 RVs. (n.d.). *What's watt? How to calculate watt hours*. https://www.solar4rvs.com.au/buying/buyer-guides/assessing-your-solar-needs/calculating-watt-hours-wh-kwh/

Svarc, J. (2019, December 19). *Top 7 solar myths busted*. Clean energy reviews. https://www.cleanenergyreviews.info/blog/top-myths-about-solar-panels

Talens Peiró, L., Villalba Méndez, G., & Ayres, R. U. (2013). *Lithium: Sources, production, uses, and recovery outlook.* JOM, 65(8), 986–996. https://doi.org/10.1007/s11837-013-0666-4

Unbound Solar. (2020, July 8). *Grid-tied vs. off-grid solar: which is right for you?* https://unboundsolar.com/blog/grid-tied-vs-off-grid-solar

Wallender, L. (2020, July 10). *The difference between watts vs. volts.* The Spruce. https://www.thespruce.com/the-difference-between-watts-vs-volts-4767057

Weir, M. (2018, July 18). *The complete guide to solar panel mounts for boats (and where to position them)* BetterBoat. https://betterboat.com/boating/solar-panel-mounts-for-boats/